Antioch Community High School
Library
1133 S. Main Street
Antioch, IL 60002

Lake Monsters

Other books in the Fact or Fiction? series:

Lake
Monsters

Fact or Fiction?

Paul Shovlin, *Book Editor*

Bruce Glassman, *Vice President*
Bonnie Szumski, *Publisher*
Helen Cothran, *Managing Editor*

OPPOSING
VIEWPOINTS®
SERIES

GREENHAVEN PRESS
An imprint of Thomson Gale, a part of The Thomson Corporation

THOMSON

GALE

Detroit • New York • San Francisco • San Diego • New Haven, Conn.
Waterville, Maine • London • Munich

For more information, contact
Greenhaven Press
27500 Drake Rd.
Farmington Hills, MI 48331-3535
Or you can visit our Internet site at http://www.gale.com

Cover credit: Chris Butler/Science Photo Library. An Elasmosaurus, a marine dinosaur, comes ashore possibly to lay its eggs.

LIBRARY OF CONGRESS CATALOGING-IN-PUBLICATION DATA
Lake monsters / Paul Shovlin, book editor.
p. cm. — (Fact or fiction?)
Includes bibliographical references and index.
ISBN 0-7377-1894-3 (lib. : alk. paper)
1. Monsters. 2. Lake animals. I. Shovlin, Paul. II. Fact or fiction? (Greenhaven Press)
QL89.L35 2005
001.944—dc22   2004055252

Printed in the United States of America

Contents

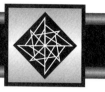

Foreword

"There are more things in heaven and earth, Horatio, than are dreamt of in your philosophy."
—William Shakespeare, *Hamlet*

"Extraordinary claims require extraordinary evidence."
—Carl Sagan, *The Demon-Haunted World*

Almost every one of us has experienced something that we thought seemed mysterious and unexplainable. For example, have you ever known that someone was going to call you just before the phone rang? Or perhaps you have had a dream about something that later came true. Some people think these occurrences are signs of the paranormal. Others explain them as merely coincidence.

As the examples above show, mysteries of the paranormal ("beyond the normal") are common. For example, most towns have at least one place where inhabitants believe ghosts live. People report seeing strange lights in the sky that they believe are the spaceships of visitors from other planets. And scientists have been working for decades to discover the truth about sightings of mysterious creatures like Bigfoot and the Loch Ness monster.

There are also mysteries of magic and miracles. The two often share a connection. Many forms of magical belief are tied to religious belief. For example, many of the rituals and beliefs of the voodoo religion are viewed by outsiders as magical practices. These include such things as the alleged Haitian voodoo practice of turning people into zombies (the walking dead).

There are mysteries of history—events and places that have been recorded in history but that we still have questions about today. For example, was the great King Arthur a real king or merely a legend? How, exactly, were the pyramids built? Historians continue to seek the answers to these questions.

Then, of course, there are mysteries of science. One such mystery is how humanity began. Although most scientists agree that it was through the long, slow process of evolution, not all scientists agree that indisputable proof has been found.

Subjects like these are fascinating, in part because we do not know the whole truth about them. They are mysteries. And they are controversial—people hold very strong and opposing views about them.

How we go about sifting through information on such topics is the subject of every book in the Greenhaven Press series Fact or Fiction? Each anthology includes articles that present the main ideas favoring and challenging a given topic. The editor collects such material from a variety of sources, including scientific research, eyewitness accounts, and government reports. In addition, a final chapter gives readers tools to analyze the articles they read. With these tools, readers can sift through the information presented in the articles by applying the methods of hypothetical reasoning. Examining these topics in this way adds a unique aspect to the Fact or Fiction? series. Hypothetical reasoning can be applied to any topic to allow a reader to become more analytical about the material he or she encounters. While such reasoning may not solve the mystery of who is right or who is wrong, it can help the reader separate valid from invalid evidence relating to all topics and can be especially helpful in analyzing material where people disagree.

Introduction

"Thus, God created the huge sea-beasts, and all the different kinds of life and movement that spring from the waters."
—Genesis 1:21

Stories of water monsters have circulated throughout recorded history. From Nahuelito of Argentina to the Turkish monster of Lake Van, from North America's Flathead Lake monster to Issie of Japan's Lake Ikeda, tales of lake monsters have persisted for centuries.

In the Western world, the Loch Ness monster, or Nessie, is probably the most famous of all lake monsters. Nessie stories date back to the sixth century, when Saint Columba, an early Christian missionary, is said to have tangled with the beast. Columba was in Scotland converting the pagans when he supposedly came upon the monster. Inhabitants of the area complained of the monster's activity, and Columba ordered one of his faithful to swim across the lake. As the follower swam across, the monster rose out of the loch and began to move ominously toward the poor swimmer. As the spectators watched aghast, Columba raised his arms and commanded the monster to cease its attack and depart. The monster roared in anger, but swam away quickly, successfully challenged by Columba's faith.

In the east, in Russia's Lake Brosno area, monster tales have circulated as early as the eighth century. The monster supposedly routed an enemy army as it prepared to invade Russia. The Lake Brosno monster reportedly scared the soldiers to death.

Lake monster phenomena are not just a remnant of our

superstitious past, however. Reports of lake monsters still filter in from all over the world. Believers attempt to develop theories and discover evidence that will prove once and for all that lake monsters exist. Critics try just as hard to show that believers are wrong. The scientific method has become an important tool on both sides to prove the argument.

The fact that lake monster stories are so persistent is an argument in favor of their existence, many believers argue. By popular accounts, lake monsters exist in the hundreds, with well over three hundred lakes rumored to be their homes. Eyewitness accounts number in the thousands, maybe in the tens of thousands. If eyewitness accounts are good enough in courts of law, supporters contend, then proof of lake monsters already exists.

Cryptozoologists (people who study hidden or unknown animals) search for unknown animals that may be at the heart of unexplainable phenomena. In the case of lake monsters, cryptozoologists claim that photographs and motion pictures support the case for lake monsters. Cryptozoologists also rely on sophisticated watercrafts, radar, sensitive sound recorders, different types of cameras, and other evolving technologies. Bob Rines's three-week-long expedition to the Loch Ness in 1999 is a case in point. The Loch Ness is twenty-four miles long and eight hundred feet deep. Rines outfitted his expedition's boats with sonar and global positioning systems to track any underwater targets. While many targets were located, the lake is so big that it was difficult to identify the fast-moving targets. Rines noted that some of the moving targets could have been schools of fish, but the study was inconclusive because many targets were unidentifiable. The Loch Ness monster could have been "the one that got away."

Other obstacles complicate the cryptozoologists' task.

Some of the lakes are inaccessible or are in inhospitable locations. Many of the lakes are large, deep, or have hidden underwater caves and caverns. The sophisticated equipment it takes to properly scan such locales can be quite expensive. Few searchers have been able to raise the money to purchase such equipment. Often, too, such scans are difficult to carry out because of the size and depth of the lakes. Even with sonar, it might take a fleet of boats, each outfitted with the appropriate equipment, to survey a lake.

For all the work cryptozoologists and other believers put in during the search for lake monsters, they have been unable to prove that the monsters exist. Critics have posed counterarguments to match those of believers. And, finally, no undeniable proof in the form of the body of a live or dead lake monster has surfaced.

Questions of scientific validity are often at the heart of debates between believers and critics. Critics often claim that monster hunters are poor scientists and that cryptozoology is a fringe science. Critics argue that no hard evidence proves that lake monsters exist. In addition, they attempt to develop their own theories to explain the phenomena that have been mistaken for lake monster activity.

Critics especially take issue with the idea that eyewitness accounts are valid proof of monsters' existence. Opponents claim that eyewitnesses are often unreliable. Studies have been performed that show that many people, especially those who are in an excited state, are unable to give accurate accounts of events they have just witnessed. In the case of lake monster sightings, often the conditions of the sightings can contribute to unreliability. Many sightings occur in poor light, too quickly, or from long distances. Under such conditions, it is hard to tell exactly what people are seeing.

Critics also point out that some witnesses will intentionally make up a story about a lake monster sighting. First, the claim will bring attention to the witness, who can boast that he or she is the one who finally obtained a sighting or picture. Rewards have been offered for pictures of lake monsters, so money can be a factor in fake photographs. Lake monster sightings can also generate wealth in the form of tourism. Lakes in which monsters have been photographed or sighted may attract visitors, who will spend their money in nearby towns. Critics argue that some cryptozoologists may falsify or misrepresent data because they stand to gain continued funding for their search for fame.

Also, critics counter, witnesses may just make mistakes. A duck, otter, or even a floating log may appear to be a lake monster from a distance. For example, during the escalation of Nessie sightings in the 1930s, researchers pointed out that tar-covered barrels bobbing in the lake from road construction may have been mistaken for the monster.

While arguing that eyewitness reports are not sufficiently scientific, critics develop theories that they claim are more likely explanations for lake monster phenomena. Scientists have explained that sightings have been the results of seismic disturbances on the lake bottoms, a strange form of waves, or merely light distortion. They argue that since these explanations have a known scientific basis, they are more plausible than some undiscovered animal.

With all the contradictions that come with this debate, making up one's mind about the existence of lake monsters is a difficult endeavor. The difficulty of this process is compounded by the fact that eyewitness sightings and photographs are virtually all one has to go on. No hard evidence, in the form of the body of an actual lake monster, exists. In spite of that, a large body of writing exists, on both sides, detailing this enigma. A careful study of the research with a critical eye is necessary to draw conclusions in this matter.

Chapter 1

Fact or Fiction?

The Lake Monsters Are Real

Numerous and Credible Sightings Prove That the Monster of Lake Brosno Exists

Sofya Vorotyntseva

Brosnya, a dinosaur or dragonlike creature, may dwell in Lake Brosno in Russia. Russia, a land with many ancient lakes, lays claim to several lake monsters. This monster has reportedly been around since the 700s. Like other monsters that have legends surrounding them, Brosnya has had many sightings over the years. *Caravan and Me*, a Russian newspaper, recently sent an expedition to Lake Brosno to search for Brosnya. Although the expedition turned up no concrete evidence for Brosnya's existence, the three reporters seem convinced that the lake has a strange inhabitant. *Pravda*, another well-known Russian newspaper, published this article, which chronicles the tales told about Brosnya. Sofya Vorotyntseva, a correspondent for *Pravda*, wrote up the report, which ran in *Pravda*'s online version on January 20, 2004.

The weekly [periodical] *Karavan + Ya* (*Caravan and Me*) published in the Russian city of Tver became widely popular seven years ago when it was first to report about a monster from Lake Brosno in the Andreapol District of the Tver Region. After the first publication in the weekly, the news about a dinosaur from Brosno spread all over the world. Journalists from Moscow and from abroad were seeking sensational publications about the monster from the Russian province. Hundreds of publications and TV programs about the Brosno monster made the creature a world sensation. The Tver weekly, *Karavan* from time to time organizes small expeditions to Lake Brosno to visit the mysterious creature that became so much popular thanks to the newspaper.

Numerous witnesses say that they saw a head of a big beast above water that looked like a dinosaur or a dragon head and a long thin tail. The people said that the creature was covered with scales like a reptile and was about five meters long.

Positive Reports from Sonar

Experts of the Kosmopoisk research association went for an expedition to Lake Brosno together with *Karavan* in the summer of 2002 and did echo deep sounding. Vadim Chernobrov, the Kosmopoisk coordinator, said in an interview to the Moscow newspaper *Argumenty i Facty* (*Arguments and Facts*): "Echo deep sounding registered an anomaly. There was a huge jelly-like mass of a railway car size hanging five meters above the bottom. The mass stood motionless. We waited for some time and then decided to make it move: we threw an underwater petard, a low capacity explosive device. When the device blew up, the creature started slowly going up. We stared at the water, and it was clear; there was nothing resembling a monster; however something unusual was still felt in the lake water."

Researchers, who believe that a mysterious big creature does live in Lake Brosno and who work on the mystery of the creature, say that Brosnya (this is the name given to the monster) cannot be a reptile. Otherwise, it would be frozen and [have] died in the climate of the middle geographic zone when dormant. If the strange creature has come to life, it means it is a mammal and breeds through syngenesis [sexual reproduction, requiring at least two creatures]. However, some problems arise in this connection. First of all, the lake is too small for an entire population of large predators to live and breed there. Second, a group of these big mysterious creatures needs much food, which is also a problem in the small lake. There is a hypothesis saying that some water systems join lakes, seas and oceans. If so, Scotland's Nessy may be a relative to Brosnya living in Russia's province.

An Old Monster

It is rumored that the strange giant creature has been living in Lake Brosno for several centuries already. One of the legends says that the lake monster scared to death the Tatar-Mongol army that headed for Novgorod in the 8th century. [Tatar-Mongol leader] Baty-khan stopped the troops to have some rest on the sides of Lake Brosno. Horses were let to drink water from the lake. However, when horses came down to the lake, a huge creature emerged from the water roaring and started devouring horses and soldiers. The Baty-khan troops were so terrified that they turned back, and

Novgorod was saved. Old legends say that some enormous mouth devoured fishermen. Chronicles mention some "sand mountain" that emerged above the lake surface from time to time. Once, Varangians [Scandinavian invaders] wanted to hide stolen treasures in the lake. But when they approached the small island, a dragon came to the surface from the lake and swallowed the small island up.

The terrible monster disturbed people's minds over the 18–19th century. It was rumored that the giant creature emerged on the lake surface in the evenings, but immediately submerged when people approached. It is said that during [World War II] the beast swallowed up a Fascist [Axis] plane. Today, there are lots of witnesses who say they chanced to see Brosnya walking in the water. People say that it turns boats upside-down and has to do with disappearance of people.

Brosnya Is Real, Say Locals

Everything said by locals and tourists who witnessed Brosnya proves that the creature (either a dragon or a dinosaur) does exist. However, some people treat the issue skeptically and still say that the creature may be a mutant beaver or a giant pike of 100–150 years. Others conjecture that groups of wild boars and elks cross the lake from time to time. Do boars and elks dive and stay under water for a long time? However, local people witnessed neither boars, nor elks.

Skeptics' Dismissals

There are some more scientific hypotheses concerning Brosnya. One of them is a gas version saying that when hydrogen sulphide goes up from the lake bottom it makes water boil up; this boiling in its turn resembles a dragon head. But the amount of hydrogen sulphide must be considerable to produce this effect. [Another] version says that there is a volcano in Lake Brosno that makes ejections on the water surface from time to time. It is well-known that there are several fractures at the bottom of the lake; the depth and the direction of the fractures cannot be defined. It is not ruled out that the volcano crater is inside of one of the fractures. This explains why the volcano, if it actually exists, has not been discovered yet.

Fishermen say that the underwater world of Lake Brosno has a structure of several levels. From time to time burbots and perch can be found in the lake. . . . For example, herring can be found in a lake in Peno District in the Tver Region. This is strange that the sea fish may live in the lake at all. Smelt shoals from time to time can be found in Lake Brosno as well. The phenomenon of Brosnya can be explained from the physical point of view: huge smelt shoals are reflected on the water surface through refraction of light and produce the effect of a huge reptile head. Physicists say that any mirage appears in hot weather. Indeed, witnesses say that they came across Brosnya in summer. However, [the] origin of the strange monster is still a mystery.

The Newspaper's Expedition

In November 1996, the *Karavan* weekly started an expedition to Lake Brosno in the Tver Region. The expedition consisted of writer and journalist from Tver Yeugeny Novikov, head of the Tver Regional Legislative Assembly's press-service Nikolay Ishchuk, journalist Marina Gavrishenko, photographer Anaida Jilavyan and editor-in-chief of the *Karavan* newspaper Gennady Klimov. . . .

Three Views on Brosnya

Gennady Klimov says:

> The lake actually keeps some secrets. When the depth of Lake Brosno was measured, it turned out that in some parts it was

120–160 meters deep. It means that Lake Brosno is the deepest in Europe. What is more, the lake belongs to the preglacial epoch; that is why mysterious phenomena are quite possible in it. As for me, my concerns about the whole of the story are quite particular. I am interested in the mechanism according to which global myths arise. I say that the administration of the Andreapol District where the lake is situated could have been more adroit to form economy of the district depending upon the Brosnya myth. Today, I do not personally care if the creature exists or not. But this is a really precious myth from the point of view of the future. Much is spoken about monster called Brosnya in different parts of Russia and in other countries, but nothing is said here in the Tver Region where the creature "lives." It is believed that Loch Ness creature does exist. The whole of the county where it lives is connected with the creature myth. . . .

Marina Gavrishenko, the journalist who took part in the expedition, says:

At first sight, the whole of the monster story looks like a fairytale. After the expedition to Lake Brosno, I do believe that the place is actually mysterious. Stories told by witnesses prove this opinion. We met with local people who were perfectly sane and adequate. What is more, all legends about the mysterious monster trace the roots back to the old times. I am sure that legends and rumors cannot arise from nothing.

Nikolay Ischuk, the head of the Tver Regional Legislative Assembly press-service, says:

I do not believe in wonders. What we chanced to see at Lake Brosno is actually mysterious and incomprehensible. If the phenomenon can be explained with the laws of the planet's life, I believe this is a miracle indeed. I recollect our expedition to Lake Brosno and our attempts to take pictures of the creature as a wonderful journey. This is wonderful that people may have such interesting adventures. May it be so that the expedition actually came across some miracle? Inexplicable things must exist in this world. When people do not understand some things they want to know more and reveal more new facts.

The Loch Ness "Monster" Is a Group of Long-Necked Seals

Peter Costello

Stories have long been told of a large monster residing in the depths of Loch Ness, Scotland. The earliest sighting is often claimed to be that of Saint Columba, in A.D. 565, who reportedly clashed with the monster while converting people in the area. In the last hundred years, "Nessie" sightings have been on the increase. In the following selection, Peter Costello suggests that Nessie is actually a group of ten to fifteen long-necked seals, a species of seal yet unknown to science. He argues that the shy nature of this undiscovered species explains the lack of physical evidence. Costello, a researcher, drew on many resources, including trips to Loch Ness, in preparing for his book *In Search of Lake Monsters*, from which the following article is excerpted.

Though it has been clear from the beginning at Loch Ness that we have been searching out one particular type of animal, several others have got mixed into the matter. For the most part these have been clearly different. Many of the Bunyips of Australia are seals of ordinary kinds. Some of the Russian reports from Siberia refer to what must be large ceteceans [whales, dolphins, or porpoises]. The buru of Assam, if that mystery beast still exists, is some kind of primitive crocodile. Only the sirrush comes close to being the archaetypical monstrous reptile of popular imagination—and what that might have been is still something of a mystery. When these are separated out—along with the odd Irish monsters such as the carabuncle—we are left with a large long-necked animal. It is that we have now finally to identify [sic].

The problem is best approached by going back to Loch Ness where we began and to its particular animals. By this time—if this were one of those old-fashioned detective novels—all the clues would be in the reader's hand. . . . It only remains to draw them together, filling out the details with the evidence from other places when necessary.

Many Guesses About the Monster's Identity

What have people imagined the Loch Ness animal to be? Well, back in the 1930's, they thought it was nearly everything under the sun. [Retired naval officer and writer Rupert] Gould, in his book, lists all the suggestions which he had been able to find, and which did not stand scrutiny: aquatic birds, salmon, otters, porpoises, plesiosaurs, tortoises, sunfish, rays, catfish, salamanders, turtles, sharks, eels, ribbon-fish, beluga (and other whales), sturgeon, squid, crocodiles, seals (including walrus, sea-lion, sea-

elephant). A long and inclusive list, of which only the plesiosaur is still put forward. None of the others will fit the
bill at all.

Today the main theories are fewer. There is the fish theory, that the monster is some species of giant eel. This seems
to have been generally abandoned after having had something of a vogue in the 1950's. Though it might explain the
humps so often seen, an eel of any size would not have a
long neck.

That the monster might be an invertebrate, some sort of
spineless giant sea-slug was suggested by [Nessie hunter and
writer] F.W. Holiday. Inherently improbable in the first
place, it does not seem to me to cover all the reports, or all
the details of the evidence, such as the mane and fur so often mentioned.

Gould's theory that the Loch Ness monster could be a
form of vastly enlarged newt attracted the support of only
one well-known scientist at the time. While it had its attractions, again it explains too little of the evidence.

The plesiosaur theory, which appeared early on, still has
many supporters. And indeed, with its long neck and flippers, the plesiosaur was a very attractive explanation. But
again the difficulties, whether it could have survived for 60
million years undetected, whether it could live in a cold
freshwater lake, are very great.

The Monster Is a Mammal

In fact the only theory that really seems to fit all the facts as
we have them is that the monster is a warm-blooded mammal. Why this should ever have been a matter of doubt is
difficult to understand. Perhaps because of pre-conceived
ideas that the sea-serpent was a plesiosaur, some assumed,
as many still do, that the monster was as well. Yet the details
of the evidence never supported such an idea.

It is difficult to envisage a reptile surviving in the cold temperate conditions of Loch Ness, or most of the other lakes where sightings have been made. Only a mammal with a fur coat and warm blood is really suited to such an environment. Even in the earliest reports, such as those from the 1880's, witnesses mentioned that the animal had hair or a mane, which only a mammal would have.

These facts were clear enough to the anti-monster critics of the 1930's. But having reasoned thus far, many scientists concluded that the most suitable mammal to explain the reports would be a seal. But no known seal has the long neck which is the distinctive feature of the animal.

Theory—the Monster Is a Seal

Only [Dutch zoologist A.C.] Oudemans, writing in Holland, took the next step of suggesting the monster was an unknown long-necked seal, an animal which would cover all the points of the evidence. True his animal has a long tail, but this notion was based on confusing reports of different types of sea-serpents. Having settled the question of the animal's basic nature, what else do we know about it?

The long-neck is a large animal, much larger than any of the seals to which it is related.

Photos Support Seal Hypothesis

The head is small and flat, with a conical muzzle which lengthens with age. In some young animals it seems to be little wider than the neck, though in older specimens it is long enough to recall the shape of a horse's head. These differences can be seen in the photographs by Kenneth Wilson [London surgeon, photographer of famous "Surgeon's Photo"], showing the muzzle, and those by F.C. Adams [Londoner, amateur photographer] where none is visible. The mouth, though seldom seen, is wide. The eyes are small, little more than narrow oval slits high on the head. The lighter colouring around the eye socket often gives the impression that the eyes are much larger than they actually are. Small "horns" have been noticed on the top of the head (again these can be seen in the Wilson photograph): these are actually ears which the animal usually lays back flat on the neck, where they have been mistaken for a sort of frill.

The long neck is the animal's distinctive and identifying feature. Narrow behind the head, it widens to the shoulders and is strongly muscled. A mane or crest is mentioned on some animals, most probably the males: what could be more appropriate for a water-horse than a mane!

The body is large and heavy, much larger than that of most seals, thick and barrel-shaped. The animal is covered in fat, and shows two or three dorsal humps, caused by the rolling up of the fat under loose folds of skin. It has been suggested that these humps are inflatable air-sacs, functioning as hydrostatic tanks to aid diving, but on the present evidence they seem to be structural.

The humps have been the cause of much discussion, yet there should be no mystery about them at all, as one of Gould's witnesses actually observed how they change shape, and drew clearly for him the various aspects of the monster. On May Day 1934 Miss Kathleen MacDonald of Inverness saw the monster on the loch [lake] between Lochend and Abriachan; it was then a "brownish drab-coloured hump". This single hump then flattened out till there was a large central hump with a smaller one fore and aft. An even smaller hump then appeared in front of the main body, which proved to be the animal's head and neck when lifted clear of the water. Beside the smaller humps there was a continuous splashing and kicking. As the animal moved forward a short distance, there was a swirl of water at the rear end, which Miss MacDonald assumed was made by a powerful tail. What could be clearer or less mysterious. So much for the humps.

Along the animal's back, the spinal vertebrae are emphasised by a crest of darker hair.

There is little or no tail, perhaps a mere stump. A careful examination of the 11 per cent of the reports that mention a "tail" show that the references are only in the most general terms. Observing movement in the water at the rear end, most witnesses, like Miss MacDonald above, assume the existence of a tail. No-one, except perhaps [medical student] Arthur Grant, has even seen the monster's tail, and I believe he was mistaken about some of what he saw that dark night in January 1934. Against this we have the evidence of such witnesses as Mrs. MacLennan at Loch Ness and Miss Carbury in Connemara that the animal's "tail resembled that of a fish", that it has "a divided, a V-shaped tail": which seem to describe rear flippers rather than an actual tail. So much for the powerful tail.

There are four webbed feet, on which the digits are large and clearly visible, sometimes giving the impression of three claws, or even of a cloven hoof. These details have been noted by [E.H.] Bright in 1880, Mrs. MacLennan in 1933 and by Bob Duff in 1969. My conclusion is also based on the appearance of the long-necks shown on the mosaic at Lydney Hall and on Arthur Grant's version of his animal's flippers. The three-toed tracks found on the beach where that animal went down into the loch are consistent with this. And with the animal being a seal-like creature.

> You will notice [writes Bernard Héuvelmans, a pioneer of cryptozoology, the scientific study of hidden species] that in all hind flippers of seals, digits I and V are the longest and best developed, and that the three inner digits are smaller and closely webbed, as if they were just one large wrinkled toe. This gives the whole flipper a three-toed aspect. Something like this:

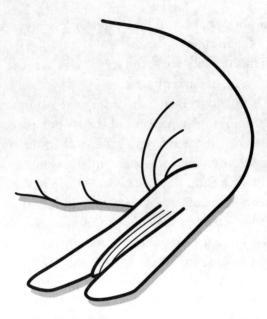

When the flipper is broadly spread out like a fin it looks a little like this:

and seen from a distance suggests a three-toed rather than a five-toed limb.

Hence the "cloven hoof" seen by Mrs. MacLennan, and the three digits seen by Bob Duff and E.H. Bright.

The front pair of flippers are often seen. The rear pair, when pointing backwards, are frequently mistaken for a tail. When spread out, however, they have the appearance of a fishtail. Both sets of limbs are used in swimming, the front pair for balance, the rear for propulsion, as is the case with the walrus. The front pair are supported by a massive sternum which gives the animal a bulky appearance. As with the walrus and the sea-lions, the limbs are adapted for use on land, where the animal moves with considerable speed and agility.

The skin is covered with a very light fur which appears smooth and glossy when wet, but rough and wrinkled when dry or seen close to. The animal is a dark brown colour, and when wet often seems black or even olive green, with a lighter underbelly and a white slash down the throat. Some younger individuals are much lighter, an almost sandy camel colour.

The size of the animals seen in Loch Ness over the years has ranged from 18 to 30 feet, the pair photographed by P.A. MacNab being representative of these sizes. The size of the animals has inevitably been exaggerated by witnesses assuming the animal has a long tail and extrapolating the real length from the visible parts. Most estimates of length ought perhaps to be reduced by a third. I doubt if most of them grow larger than 20 feet overall. The large animal in the MacNab photo is probably the old bull that has frightened several witnesses over the years.

The Nature of the Long-Necked Seal

As these animals are shy and retiring, few details of their behaviour are known. They are most often seen in bright calm summery weather, showing a preference for warm days.

However, such weather is more likely to bring out people than monsters, for they have been reported not merely in the summer, but at all seasons of the year, even in the middle of winter snow storms.

Many witnesses are struck by their turn of speed, which is quite considerable, over 20 knots at times. The implication of this is that they feed on fast swimming fish, and what little is known of their movements about the loch confirms that they feed on the shoals of fish at river mouths and close to the banks. Their long flexible neck is well adapted to this existence.

Like seals, they use echo-location to trace their prey. This dependence on sonar may well be due to their being partially sighted, or even blind, from living in the dark gloom of the loch. As a consequence the animal's hearing is exceptionally sharp. . . .

The animal's breath has been observed once—from its mouth— . . . by a naturalist. Its peculiar habit of lying motionless on the surface of the water suggests that it hyperoxygenates its bloodstream before lengthy dives. Seals do this as well: it has been found that Weddell's seal [a species of Antarctic seal] can dive to depths of 250 fathoms [1 fathom = about 6 feet], remain down for half an hour and travel 20 miles under the ice without surfacing to breathe.

The animal dives swiftly, often straight down. Its other peculiar habit of rolling around on the surface may be to rid itself of parasites.

Though not reported from Loch Ness since 1923, these animals have a sharp staccato cry, much resembling a sea-lion's bark.

Nothing as yet is known about the reproduction, birth, growth or maturity of these animals. We can assume, however, that to maintain a population in Loch Ness, a herd of at least 15 to 20 animals must exist there.

The Seals Do Not Live Only in Loch Ness

These animals are found in many other steep-shored lakes in the cold temperate regions of the Northern and Southern Hemispheres, roughly in a band on either side of the 10°C isotherms. Often these are lakes in alpine mountain areas, but they are also found in rivers and marshes. Appropriately enough, in the Italian Alps Lake Maggiore is the reputed haunt of a monster. In 1934 fishermen reported they had seen it where the River Ticino runs into the lake. It was not however dreamed up just to cash in on the fashion for monsters, because this particular monster—said to have a horse's head and to live on fish—was mentioned at the beginning of the 19th century in one of his travel books by the novelist Stendhal. . . .

A Zoological Proposal

In summary: the Loch Ness animal (and its relations) is a large long-necked [seal], more specialised for a purely aquatic existence than any known seal. (It has reached the stage of giving birth in the water, which seals are only infrequently forced into doing.) The scientific name proposed for this animal is *Megalotaria longicollis*, "the big sea-lion with a long-neck", which was suggested by Bernard Héuvelmans in 1965. This name has not been generally adopted however, due partly to doubts still remaining with many zoologists about the existence of the animal, even though the evidence is so overwhelming.

Why this should be so is perhaps the only really mysterious feature of this whole affair. But as a minor prophet ought to have said at sometime or other: the mind of the scientist is exceedingly strange, who can know it?

Lake Erie's Monster Could Be a Giant Sturgeon

Ron Schaffner

North America hosts many lakes that are reputed to be the domains of lake monsters. People have allegedly sighted something in the depths of Ohio's Great Lake, Lake Erie. Ron Schaffner, an amateur cryptozoologist, chronicles some of the sightings of the monster, "South Bay Bessie." Schaffner composes a list of the characteristics of South Bay Bessie as noted by eyewitnesses. He then posits that the creature could, in fact, be a rare species of fish, a giant lake sturgeon. Although lake sturgeons were abundant in the area in the mid-1800s, they are now endangered and considered quite rare. Sturgeons can grow as heavy as two hundred pounds. Schaffner's article originally appeared in the *North American Biofortean Review*, a journal dedicated to cryptozoology, the search for undiscovered species of animals.

When dealing with topics such as cryptozoology, we rely heavily on reports from the media and eyewitness encounters. This testimony can lead to various problems when evaluating a report and the investigator has to make a determination if the story told is not a misinterpretation or a fallacy. The old cliché that all legends have a basis in fact is not always true. Many legends may be nothing more than a campsite story passed down through the generations.

I was introduced to an interesting story while publishing my newsletter, *Creature Chronicles*, back in 1991. A correspondent sent me various newspaper clippings from the *Ottawa County (Ohio) Beacon*. The editor had been collecting reports of some sort of serpent reported in the western basin of Lake Erie. From the reports I received, a story was developing about a strange creature similar to that of Loch Ness and the Ogopogo monster.

This animal had been dubbed the name South Bay Bessie by some of the locals from a contest that was held promoting lakeside tourist attractions. The basic description was that of a 30–50 foot long snake-like animal about as round as a bowling ball. The reported creature seems to appear when the water is calm. Reports of this water creature date back some thirty years.

A Chronicle of Sightings

For simplicity of this article, allow me to cite a few reports from the past, so that the reader may become familiar with this alleged creature:

1960—Ken Golic was fishing off a pier in Sandusky when he heard two rats. He decided to throw a couple of rocks at them when he saw the creature. He stated that it was cigar-shaped and came out of the water about 1–1½ feet. It was about 11:00 P.M. on a clear, calm night.

1969—Jim Schindler stated that a serpent came within 6 feet of him near South Bass Island. Although he did not see the length, the width was about 2 feet. The animal appeared to be about 1 foot under the water.

9/1981—Theresa Kovach of Akron saw a snake-like reptile that "was so large that [it] could [have] easily capsized a boat. It seemed to be playing." She watched it from a house on the Cedar Point Causeway.

1983 (app.)—Mary M. Landoll told John Schaffner about her encounter with Bessie off Rye Beach in Huron. Mary went out to the front porch just before dawn when the lake was quite placid. From the left end, she heard a rowing sound and saw what looked like a capsized boat. It was a greenish-brown color about 40–50 feet in length. Landoll realized that it wasn't a boat, but an animal of some sort. It had a long neck and an eye was visible on the side of the head with a grin going up one side. The creature appeared to be playing in the water, but still put a scare into the witness.

Summer, 1985—Tony Schill of Avon, Ohio, was boating with friends north of Vermilion when they reported the serpent. It was dark brown and had a flat tail. Tony stated that "5 humps came out of the water. No way it was a sturgeon."

Dale Munro, of Lorain was also boating when he came face-to-face with it. He stated that it had 3 humps and was black. He also reported that it was twice the size of his 16-foot boat. The location was in calm waters just off the Lorain Coast Guard Station and his sighting lasted 3–4 minutes.

May or June, 1989—Gail Kasner obtains a graph from a boat owned by Ken Smith, of Streetsboro. The fish finder appears to show a sonar reading of a cigar-shape apparition about 35 feet in length at a depth of about 30 feet.

July 8, 1990—Susan Seeson of Salem witnessed the creature 2 miles from Cedar Point. Her description basically matched other reports.

September 3, 1990—Bob Soracco was jet skiing off Port Clinton when he thought he spotted a porpoise. (Porpoise in fresh water? Oh well, Bob had just moved from Florida.) He told reporters that he saw humps with gray spots. "It was very long as I moved closer and it was going down."

September 4, 1990—Harold Bricker and his family were fishing north of Cedar Point Amusement Park when a serpent type creature swam by their boat about 1000 feet away. Their description—35 feet long with a snake-like head. It moved as fast as their boat. Later, the Brickers reported their sighting to the [Ohio Department of Natural Resources] ODNR rangers at East Harbor State Park.

September 11, 1990—Fire inspectors, Jim Johnson and Steve Dircks, of Huron saw the creature from a third story window facing Lake Erie. They described it as dark blue or black at about 30–45 feet long. [One] further stated that he saw three parts of the creature above water. "It laid there motionless for three to six minutes and was flat on top."

Week of September 16, 1991—Dennis Szececinski of Toledo saw Bessie near Toledo's water intake structure three miles offshore in Maumee Bay. He was fishing in the bay when something long and black slithered in front of him. . . .

Reports of Bessie Proliferate

During the years of 1992–1994, I took a leave of absence from my research, as I returned to college. I put 'Bessie' on the back burner until I could return to the world of cryptozoology. In 1997, I added my original story to my web page.

To my surprise, I was receiving a large amount of email regarding this subject. Some of these posts appeared to have some merit, but I still wasn't convinced that there was a serpent in Lake Erie. Nevertheless, I put the reports up on my web site in hopes that I could get a better understanding of the phenomenon.

A Video Is Taken of South Bay Bessie

In 1991, George Repicz took some video that he believes may have been some sort of creature.

His report is as follows:

> In July 1991 my family and I spent a week at a family camp on Kelley's Island. I took my camcorder to film family events and local scenery. On one of the days during that week and after filming all over the camp, I decided to get a good sunset on film. The picture through the lens did not look that great because the camera I was using did not amplify the light like some newer ones do these days. So I decided to scan the bay for something interesting when by chance I came across this (I believe was a swimming creature) moving object in the bay. The bay at the point where I shot the film is about 1 plus miles across. Around the bay is about 3 to 5 miles. The people who were fishing or boating in the scene were close to the state campgrounds across the bay. I'm not aware if any of those people saw what I saw. The people next to me could barely see the object in the water with their eyes. The camcorder was zoomed out to max and the object appears closer than it is. When our week ended we went home. That was the last time that we went to that camp.
>
> In 1993 my mother passed away so I tried to gather all possible film clips of her to share with my brothers and sister. It so happened that the scene of the creature was also part of the overall family film that I took. By chance I saw this clip again but soon forgot about it again. I think in either 1994 or 1995 I saw a program on TV about some creature in Lake Erie. I remember seeing the wake or wave that people took pictures of that was supposed to be the creature. I remembered that at the end of the clip I took of the swimming creature was the same wake. At the end of 1997 I happened to be on the net and decided to search for sea creatures when I came across the Cryptozoology zone web site and then discovered your site.

George's video is intriguing. At this time, it appears to be driftwood, but the object clearly shows movement against the current. The film is still being analyzed. . . .

A Family Spots Bessie

The following year, I received the most recent report. It occurred in Bay Village, Ohio, and was told to me by Leslee Rasgaitis:

> On July 28th at about 7:00 P.M., we were returning to our home in Bay Village from an outing with my nephews. We stopped at Huntington Beach to show them the Great Lake Erie. They are from Charleston, South Carolina. The youngest one wanted to go down to the beach and touch the fresh water, and see if he could see Canada. Meanwhile, my husband and son stayed at the top of the cliffs that overlook the lake and viewed from there, a very long, rippling, effect in the water. While watching the effect, it took on a more physical appearance, and soon they were able to see three distinct black humps rising from the water. The sun was in the west and silhouetted the thing. When I arrived from the beach they were standing watching the last of the "thing." I personally only caught a brief glimpse of something moving. But it was definitely not just a fish or a seagull.
>
> It was just about 500 feet from the shore at the end of the stone piers. It was pretty close considering it was a warm summer evening and there were still people and boats about. The actual sighting was preceded by a lot of rolling of the water; lots of bubbles and a general disturbance of pretty soft waves, which drew their attention. The sun really illuminated it. Then there was a surfacing of something VERY long and sort of roundish like a tree trunk. At first they thought it might be a tree and then it moved. They watched it for about 5–6 minutes. Rick told a friend who is an active fisherman what he had seen and was told it was probably "Bessie." I decided to look it up on the Internet and found your site. I have confirmed what I have sent you with both Rick and Victor.

Earlier Sightings

I have attempted to paint a picture for the reader that clearly shows that Lake Erie is home to some sort of aquatic creature. The reports are impressive, but we must remember the problems with witness interpretation. It is also imperative that we attempt a research endeavor going back to earlier accounts. We need to account a time line to demonstrate the Birth of Bessie up until the present.

A time line is beneficial because it presents several variables to the phenomenon. For instance, sociological and economic situations change over the years. The media's coverage of events becomes more sensationalized or downplayed depending on the mood of the populace.

The nickname of "Bessie" is relatively recent. However, reports of a serpent in Lake Erie date back to the early 1900's.

The following account supposedly occurred near Sandusky on July 21, 1931. Through this one account, the reader can see that legends of strange creatures in the western basin have been around for a long time.

"Two Cincinnati fishermen, Clifford Wilson and Francis Cogenstose, described a 'serpent' that raised out of the water along side their boat. They said the beast measured about twenty feet and was about twelve inches long at the broadest part. Even though they were frightened, they jabbed it with an oar, fastened it to a line and brought it to shore.

Several important people saw the carcass from Sandusky, including Police Captain Leo Schiverly and three newspapermen: E.L. Ways, C.J. Irwin and Mel Harman. According to the Associated Press, the creature was described as huge, snake-like and colored black, dark green and white. The hide appeared similar to an alligator."

The article mentions other reports of a sea serpent.

Unfortunately, the story doesn't mention what happened to the animal. Some researchers have dismissed the account as a hoax. It could be possible that they did capture some sort of fish species and it wasn't recognizable to them.

A More Recent Encounter

Recently, I received an email from Dave Monk of Windsor, Ontario. He explained that he had an encounter in September of 1986 while fishing the Detroit River near Peace Fountain. Dave was trolling with a pickerel jig. As he bent down to adjust his fishing line, he noticed a long, black neck appear out of the water for about 30 seconds. He further stated that this "neck" rose about seven feet above the water.

The creature submerged only to reappear a second time. At this point, Monk reeled his line and watched the animal disappear into the current heading for Lake St. Clair.

Mr. Monk goes on to report that the eyes entranced him. He felt as if the object had some sort of intelligence.

In 1990, he contacted the Great Lakes Institute and gave an account of his experience in hopes that someone could give him a logical explanation. Monk doesn't mention who he talked with, but told me that someone from the institute told him that bottom areas of the Great Lakes have never been explored.

Bessie Makes the National News

The July 29, 1993, edition of the *Wall Street Journal* wrote a skeptical piece about the phenomenon. They theorized that the reports were a marketing tool to bring tourists into the town of Huron. This northern Ohio city would become the National Live Capture and Control Center for Bessie, the Lake Erie Monster.

The reward for the capture was offered by Tom Solberg of the Huron Lagoons Marina. He was willing to pay $100,000 for the safe capture of the beast.

A Sketchy Story

In January, 1999, several messages were posted to a cryptozoology list on the Internet in regards to an incident on Lake Erie. Allegedly, Bessie was reported to have attacked a sailboat killing three people. The creature was said to have a horse-shaped head. No source was given for the incident, so I wrote several newspapers in an attempt to track down this story.

I received an informational reply from the *Sandusky Register*. Their research department informed me that this story had appeared in the tabloid newspaper *The Weekly World News* dated August 24, 1993. The cover contained a photo of a "dinosaur-like" creature wrapped around a sailboat and was allegedly taken from an airplane. However, the *Register* has no mention of any deaths.

Reporters from the *Register* had talked to the pilot, but he wished confidentiality, so I wasn't able to obtain a name. I was told that the staff did not take the report seriously and felt it was a hoax. The newspaper does have a file on Bessie, but at this time, I'm unable to make the trip to Sandusky, nor do I have the funds to pay for a search of information.

What Could Bessie Be?

I was also told that reporter Don Lee covered a "flap" of Bessie reports in 1990 and 1992. He wrote about Gary Couts of White Landing who operated "Special Lake Investigations" out of his home. Couts is said to be interested in "Bigfoot, 100-foot octopi and other interesting creatures."

Some cryptozoologists believe the entire Bessie scenario is nothing more than a hoax based on newspaper embellishments and promotional ploys. Supermarket tabloids raise more suspicions when writing feature articles on monster accounts. One can clearly see that South Bay Bessie is on the minds of the many residents along Lake Erie coast. It would be safe to say that anyone living around Lake Erie would claim a sighting of this animal when they observe something in the water that they cannot identify.

But, what if credible fishermen, boaters and lakeside observers are witnessing something unidentifiable to them? Are they seeing a lake serpent, or something else that can be explained in conventional terms? It should be noted that eyewitness observations can be fallible and not everybody interprets their observation in the same manner. They may add descriptive details in a later interview and their subconscious may have recorded a detail from a story they may have heard years ago.

Bessie May Be a Lake Sturgeon

Let's take a look at the basic descriptions and see if we can attribute this to any known species inhabiting the Great Lakes:

1. 30–50 foot snake-like or cigar-shaped
2. Reported in water which is calm
3. Width of two feet
4. Eye visible on one side of the head
5. Reported 30 feet underwater with a fish finder
6. Color described as black, brown, blue or green
7. Some witnesses describe "humps"

If we allow for some natural exaggerations on the part of the witness, it is plausible that they have misinterpreted a serpent for the endangered lake sturgeon (*Acipenser fulvescens*). Certainly, the sturgeon is prehistoric in appearance. Since this fish is rarely seen these days, the casual observer may have difficulty in identification. After all, their size can sometimes reach up to 200 pounds.

The largest lake sturgeon as recorded in [George C.] Becker's *Fishes of Wisconsin* was caught from Batchawana Bay of Lake Superior in 1921 or 1922. It was 90 inches and weighed 310 pounds. A similar catch occurred in southern Lake Michigan in 1943. That fish was 95 inches and similar in weight.

According to the Ohio Department of Natural Resources fact sheet, the sturgeon's habitat requires water with sand, gravel and rocky bottoms. This habitat is indicative of Lake Erie's bottom, especially close to shore where many sightings take place. The bony plates could be misconstrued as humps under certain conditions. The color descriptions could be the result of sunlight reflections against the clear water in the late spring.

The observance of this fish would be a rare occurrence for any knowledgeable fisherman or photographer. If you factor in the sighting by someone not familiar with this species, you could have a report of a lake serpent. Remember the problems associated with eyewitness testimony.

Perhaps this endangered species does not apply to some of the reported accounts. It is equally plausible that misinterpretations of driftwood and other debris could be mistaken for a creature. We cannot ignore any possibilities until there is a catch of Bessie and the determination is made that it is a lake sturgeon. Even then, more reports will continue to surface. . . .

For now, however, the evidence seems to indicate that the Birth of South Bay Bessie probably resulted from some fabricated newspaper reports of the past. These stories soon began a legend that could be used to heighten tourist attractions. Furthermore, with these reports circulating the shores of Lake Erie, it is no surprise that lakeshore residents and vacationers have heard the reports and seen for themselves an unusual aquatic creature swimming the lake.

As always, this writer keeps an open mind. The hoax and misinterpretation factor may not be an easy solution. I am open to any suggestions along with reports and documentation on this phenomenon.

Lake Champlain's Champ Is a Plesiosaur

True Authority.com

Vermont's Lake Champlain is believed to be the home of one of the best-known lake monsters of North America, "Champ." Supposedly, Samuel de Champlain, the explorer the lake is named for, observed Champ in the early 1600s. Since then, Champ has been sighted many times. True Authority.com, a Web site that provides a variety of perspectives on matters concerning dinosaurs, creationism and evolution, and cryptozoology, the scientific study of hidden or unknown species, describes Champ and argues that the monster is a plesiosaur. Plesiosaurs were large marine creatures that have been extinct since the time of the dinosaurs. The modern discovery of other animals thought to be extinct, like the coelacanth, a fish caught in 1938, has encouraged some monster hunters to believe that plesiosaurs could still be alive as well.

Champ, the famed sea monster of Lake Champlain. The stories surrounding this beloved animal of lore add yet another exciting chapter to cryptozoology's continuing mysteries. As with all reported unidentified lake creatures, the sightings of Champ take us far back in history, specifically to the year 1609. Yet earlier accounts exist, those given by the Indians that inhabited the land before the white man came. The tribes that lived near what is now called Lake Champlain were the Abenaki and the Iroquois. Each had its own legends concerning a creature in the lake. The Abenaki called the creature Tatoskok.

Samuel de Champlain, world famous French explorer and founder of Quebec, "discovered" the lake in 1609, when he was fighting the Iroquois in New York with his new allies, the Huron. With regards to Champ, however, he was not the first European to sight the creature as has been widely reported. Sometime during that same period, he reported seeing a monstrous creature along the coast of the St. Lawrence estuary. A journalist in 1960 inaccurately reported the location as Lake Champlain and yet another "legend" was born.

An Early Sighting

However, it was in the year 1609 that he did see the creature in Lake Champlain, and since then hundreds have been added to his number. Samuel de Champlain claimed to see an unknown animal, 11–12 meters long and about 30 cm in diameter, dark to mahogany in color, almost black and looking like a giant snake. Of course, this report fits along nicely with the hundreds of others, though many other reports don't describe the creature being "snake-like." There may be a significant explanation for this, which will be touched upon later.

A Large and Deep Lake

Lake Champlain, on the border between New York, Vermont and extending a little north into Quebec, is almost identical in structure to the many other lakes that are said to be inhabited by mysterious, large creatures. For one, it is extremely wide and extremely deep, with an area of over 490 square miles (it is the fourth largest lake in the U.S.). It reaches 13 miles in width maximum, and is up to 400 feet deep in some places. While Loch Ness reaches an approximate 754 (230m) feet deep maximum, Champlain covers much more area (Ness only has an area of about 21.8 square miles). To put it simply, it is quite possible, scientifically and logically, that unknown animals exist within the depths of the lake. Not only that, animals that most scientists would falsely dub "prehistoric."

Champ Is Obviously a Plesiosaur

If it were not for the Mansi photograph [famous photo of Champ taken in 1977], True Authority would not take such a dogmatic stance that the creature of Lake Champlain is a species of Plesiosaur. Plesiosaurs were a group of marine-dwelling reptiles (they were not true dinosaurs) that ranged in size from the 7-foot long Plesiosaurus to the 46-foot long Elasmosaurus. They possessed deep bodies, short tails, and more than the normal five bones in each finger or flipper (they often had as many as ten bones in each finger). Plesiosaurs are divided into two groups or superfamilies: those with short necks and large heads, such as Kronosaurus, which are in the superfamily Pliosauroidea; and those with long necks and small heads, such as the Elasmosaurus or Cryptoclidus, which are in the superfamily Plesiosauroidea.

Nessie seems to be that of the latter.

Though many scientists enjoy to make claims that they know a great deal about Plesiosaurs, in truth we know very little about them, as with every dinosaur ever discovered. Fossils and bones can only reveal to us so much; the rest is simply guess-work. The claim that "Champ would need to come up for air every so often" is, to simply put it, just a claim. We know nothing of Plesiosaur air capacity nor anything else about them in this regard.

Up to 1992 there have been a total of 180 witness accounts of Champ, and of these, 83 of them mention a long neck with a small head, which is the common description for lake monsters throughout the entire world. Up to a few years ago, the total individual people that claim to have seen Champ number around 600.

A Father and Daughter See Champ

Dennis Hall, a carpenter 28 years of age, says he has looked for the famed creature ever since he was 10. He said he was getting into a boat with his daughter, son and father-in-law, when his daughter spotted a creature on June 30, 1985. The creature was about a mile away when it was first seen.

Hall was about a mile from the Basin Harbor Club in Vergennes when the creature surfaced, he said. As he puts it, he didn't even know he was filming the animal until the reality of it set in.

"My daughter yelled, 'Dad, there's something out there,'" Hall said. "I have film of it for maybe 20 seconds. I can't prove it's Champ . . . but you can see it raise its neck and then lower it back into the water."

Hall said the creature was about 30 feet long, "but the neck was really thick. I've spent my whole life on or about the lake, and this is the third time I have seen it."

Hall was sitting in a canoe when he filmed the creature,

so parts of the videotape are jumbled. Though not strikingly clear, the tape does show an object protruding from the lake and moving across the surface. Hall is so convinced he has captured Champ on film that he has had the film copyrighted.

On videotape, the object appears to have two sections, and at the end of the tape, it appears to dive into the water with a large splash. The object appears to be alive, but because of distance, the videotape is difficult to make out.

According to Hall, after the animal disappeared from view, he chased after it in a motorboat. When he arrived around the bend where he saw the creature disappear, there was nothing there.

"There were no boats, the water was calm, there was nothing out there," Hall said.

Still photographs of the videotape, shot in sequence, confirm that an object is moving and its shape is changing in a snake-like motion as it goes. Hall said he videotaped the creature from about one mile, but the photographs do provide great detail.

It was the third time Hall had seen the creature. He had also seen Champ swimming near the breakwater in Burlington on June 25, from a distance of about 50 feet, in a marsh connected to Otter Creek, during the Spring of 1977.

More than One Creature

Joseph W. Zarzynski, director of the Lake Champlain Phenomena Investigation, has been studying Champ for 11 years. He says he has yet to see the creature himself, though he did see the Loch Ness monster in Scotland in the late '70s. He is convinced that there is some kind of large creature living in Lake Champlain. But, as should be the knowledge of anyone who believes in Champ, there is more than one creature in the lake. As Zarzynski put it himself, "We are talking about animals in the plural. I think we're dealing with 10 or 15 of them, a breeding colony."

Years ago, on June 29 [1977], two women called Zarzynski and claimed they saw the creature in the same spot Hall had seen it. Earlier that same day, Zarzynski, Richard Smith and Dennis Hall had been at the spot testing equipment to detect Champ. Hall had suggested to Zarzynski the location, based on theories that Hall had developed.

The women described the creature much as Hall did. Jane Temple and Peggy McGeoch, two workers at the Basin Harbor Club in Vergennes, said they saw Champ while they were at work. McGeoch said the animal raised its head and neck about five feet out of the water. She claimed the creature "was huge, about 36 inches in diameter. I thought at first I was seeing a very large fish jump, but then I saw (what I thought were) two other fish jump behind it. That's when I realized it was not a fish. There were humps. . . . Fish do not do a ballet in the water."

McGeoch also said the animal "moved like a caterpillar going across your driveway, only it was in the water. I couldn't believe what I was looking at."

More Support for Plesiosaur Theory

According to Zarzynski, Champ, from the descriptions, must be a species of plesiosaur. The Loch Ness monster is also most often explained as a plesiosaur, Zarzynski said. Zarzynski admits there are probably many sightings that are logs or scuba divers, but some people are definitely seeing something out of the ordinary. "We do have America's Loch Ness in our backyard."

Spotted Again the Next Day

Pete Horton of Bridport [Vermont] reported that he spotted a creature in Potash Bay in Addison on July 1 [1977]. The very next day a similar animal was spotted by two Delaware women near Elm Point in Addison.

"It was definitely not a fish, not an eel and not a snake," Rita Schaffer said. Lillian Cayo of St. Albans said she, her husband, her son, and a friend all saw the creature four times near their house. All the sightings, she said, occurred when the water was calm and there were no boats on the lake. It's quite interesting, because after a while, you notice the same things each time. "There isn't any noise," Cayo said. "I think the creature must know it's a good time to move about or whatever.". . .

Law Protecting Champ Lends Credence to Its Existence

The physical, actual reality of Champ of Lake Champlain is far greater than what the populace realizes. The state of Vermont passed a bill into law in 1983 which protected the creature from human harm. How much more a reality can you make of an imaginative, mythical animal? Indeed, very little, and as more tests and more expeditions are made to the famed home of Champ, the beloved monster of Vermont, the evidence will only continue to grow until, to the dismay and shock of many, Champ will be added to the growing list of our current animal kingdom.

A Monster
Exists in Lake
Memphremagog

Jacques Boisvert

Since 1798, strange rumors have been circulating near
Canada that something lurks in Lake Memphremagog.
French-Canadian Jacques Boisvert, president and founder of
the International Dracontology Society of Lake Memphremagog and the Historical Society of Lake Memphremagog,
details the life of this legend. In particular, he focuses on several eyewitness accounts, both old and new. Boisvert draws
on his vast experience scuba diving in the lake. In his article
he notes that he had no firsthand experience with Memphre,
as the lake monster is now known. Still Boisvert claims he
has an open mind and that he believes in Memphre. Perhaps
his persistence has paid off. After writing the article, he had
a brief encounter with what may have been Memphre. During a dive, he touched something large that swam off. This
article was originally published in *Crypto*, an online journal
dedicated to cryptozoology.

Lake Memphrémagog, an international lake located in Canada and the United States, 70 miles east of Montreal, straddles the United States border. The white man has been living around the lake for only two centuries. Before this, the area was favored by the Natives due to the abundance of game and fish.

Pioneers Hear Eerie Reports Near Lake Memphrémagog

The early pioneers who settled along the shores of Lake Memphrémagog were far from entertaining any thoughts that they would hear about a sea serpent in Lake Memphré-magog.

Ralph Merry is acknowledged as the first pioneer to settle in Magog (Outlet) in 1798. His son, bearing the same name, wrote in his journal dated 1816, kept at the Stanstead Historical Society, that he met eight persons who related having experienced four sightings of the sea serpent of Lake Memphrémagog. He added: *"I heared (sic) it said that Indians would not go into this lake because there were great serpents or aligators (sic) in it."* After a great deal of research, Merry's narration may be one of the oldest known in the world of Cryptozoology (science of hidden animals).

In their treatise on Geography published in 1871, The Christian Schools Brothers mentioned on page 28, concerning the animals of Québec, *"There are no rattlers; one has seen aspics, but they are extremely rare. One must not forget the large serpent named Anaconda, and which shows itself free at lake Memphrémagog."* Our ancestors learned this in school; in those days, an order of teaching brothers who published books used by pupils was taken seriously. That is to say that the tradition of an underwater monster in Lake Memphré-magog has known continuity for almost 200 years.

The Historical Society Unearths Documents

Around 1980, I started my interest in the history of the lake, intrigued by discoveries made during underwater dives. I commenced to accumulate data which brought me to found that same year *"la société d'histoire du lac Memphrémagog"* [The Historical Society of Lake Memphrémagog]. Later on I found documents relating to sightings of a creature in the lake (in French we use "apparitions," a word suggested by l'Office de la langue française du Québec). One of the earliest sightings is dated in 1847 which appeared in the *Stanstead Journal* and of which an extract follows: *"I am not aware if this is generally known that there exists in Lake Memphrémagog strange animals such as giant sea serpents or alligators etc. . . ."*

A French author, Michel Muerger, ethnologist of l'Institut Métapsychique Internationale de Paris with Claude Gagnon, BSC [Bachelor of Science], of l'Université du Québec of Montréal, wrote in 1982 a book entitled *Les monstres des lacs du Québec*, since translated in English under the title *Lake Monster Traditions* (Fortean Tomes, England, 1988). I had supplied Mr. Muerger with all the documentation that I had in my possession and it was used in an entire chapter of the book.

During the years of 1850, 1853, 1855, 1866, 1871, 1877, 1879, 1892, many newspapers reported sightings of a creature in Lake Memphrémagog.

A Convincing Sighting

On the 22nd of June 1987, I wrote to Mrs. John Webster, who was a witness to such an incident in 1935, and here is part of her reply:

> *Dr. Claussen was having a fire on the beach. It was snowing at the time, it was in October. Dr. Claussen came up to the cottage*

all excited and said: "I want you to come down and see if you two see what I do." As Mrs Claussen and I got down to the beach it (alligator type monster) was disappearing into the lake. . . . It left very large tracks. Fifty years is a long time ago.

This statement is very convincing, is it not?

A precious find is the book *Uriah Jewett and the Sea Serpent of Lake Memphrémagog* published in 1917, in Newport, Vermont. This book is very scarce although the content is very sketchy concerning sightings. Nevertheless Uriah Jewett remains a real person and legendary in the annals of our lake history.

More Lake Monster Reports

In 1983, after having completed about 1000 underwater dives I still had not found traces of the sea serpent. I then decided to write an article on the subject on the 18th of August for the *Newport Daily Express*, under the title *Lake Memphrémagog's Anacondo, a myth, a legend or a reality?* The aim was to obtain an answer or some information. The answer was not long in waiting and I received a letter from Mrs. Barbara Malloy of Newport, and here is an excerpt:

After reading your article on Magog's mystery serpent in the New-port Daily Express, I just had to write to you, relating our own phenomenal experience the day before. I, along with my two daughters . . . and she writes the description of her sighting. . . . Should we believe there is a mystery serpent in lake Memphrémagog . . . ?

I was most skeptical, but I answered her letter immediately, including a map of the lake, asking her to indicate the exact location, a drawing of the creature, and all the possible descriptions of what she had seen. The answer was not long in waiting again, together with all the pertinent data required. I telephoned her, and we set a rendezvous. After having discussed the incident for a long time, I found her most convincing.

The Word *Dracontologie* Is Coined

During that time, I pursued my research and I was in contact with a monk at the Benedictine Abbey of St-Benoît-du-Lac. I knew that the science that deals with the study of hidden animals was named cryptozoology but I wanted to find a word that would identify the science dealing with strange lake-dwelling creatures that could live in our lakes. My friend, a Benedictine friar and a linguist, found the word: *"dracontologie,"* which was officially accepted by *l'Office de la langue française du Québec* on December 3rd, 1984. We did have the English toponym (dracontology) accepted one year later by the *American Heritage Dictionary*. Starting in 1986, with a colleague in the United States, Mrs. Barbara Malloy from Newport, Vermont, we officially established *la société internationale de dracontologie du lac Memphrémagog*.

Memphré Is Named

As our creature did not have a name, we had to find one; all the names of known monsters had English names: Kelpie, Nessie, Tessie, Caddie, Champ etc. . . . I thought of "Memphré" which would become the first aquatic creature with a French name. These events took place during the time when the Canadian and American governments were negotiating the free trade deal and here in Québec, more than one person worried over losing their French identity over this treaty which became in effect on January 1st, 1989.

Mrs. Malloy and I visited the representatives of the City of Newport, Vermont, where we submitted an international cordial accord to be accepted by the Cities of Magog and Newport, which was signed on June 19, 1986, during an international press conference held in Magog under the flags of Canada, United States, Québec and Vermont.

At that time, our society had recorded 46 sightings, involving about 92 persons. Nine witnesses were present at the conference and available to journalists to confirm having seen strange things in the lake, possibly "Memphré." Since that time our creature has been a happy subject for some, mysterious for others and certainly a curiosity for all news media. Our society has worked very hard and to this day we count 182 sightings. We have always been frank in our writings and in our declarations. Those who have accused us of promoting a hoax had to suffer a retreat.

Memphré Is Protected by Law

During the first year of our society the Legislative Assembly of Vermont passed a law (#J.H.R. 19) on March 17, 1987, and adopted unanimously, for the protection of "Memphré."

A similar request was presented to the government of Québec. We have had numerous meetings with the senior civil servants involved, but up to this day there has been no action. We still hope that the government will treat our work in a more serious fashion.

William Owen, author of a book entitled the *Loch Ness Monster*, in 1984 divides his readers into groups: firm believers, those who won't believe until they are bitten by a monster, and those who retain an open mind. Quite often I have been asked if I believed in the phenomenon of "Memphré"? I rather class myself with those who have an open mind since my philosophy is thus: *"I am for everything and against nothing."* It is not because I have not seen that it does not exist.

Keeping an Open Mind

Totaling over 6000 scuba dives in the past 21 years, I have yet to encounter this intriguing and elusive friend, who knows? Maybe this year [2001] which coincides with our 15th anniversary will lead to an encounter?

In contrast, my American colleague Mrs. Malloy, has a different concept; the following is an excerpt from an article written by Peter Scowen and published in *The Stanstead Journal*, dated June 8th, 1988.

She wants positive proof of what she saw from Shattuck Hill that August evening in 1983. She goes back there in the morning, sometimes with a mug of coffee, a pair of binoculars and a camera in hopes she can put all doubts to rest. It would be nice if we were the first to scientifically document the existence of this animal. One hundred and fifty years have gone by and we're still at square one. Am I going to my grave like Uriah Jewett did? she asks. I don't want to die without documenting it, or one hundred years from now people will still be saying it's just a legend.

Times change, and the openness of mind of people makes things easier for us; they cheerfully relate to us what they have seen. It is true that our society has received an extraordinary coverage from the media such as: *"Dossiers Mystères," "On the road again," "On a pas tout vu," "On aura tout vu," "Les Tannants,"* twice with *"Reflet d'un pays," "Channel 5, Boston," "Les routes du Québec," "WCAX TV,"* and many other documentaries on this strange subject.

Five Sightings in 1995

As an example, here is a resume of the sightings for the year 1995. Our society has registered five sightings and each one involved at least two persons. I cannot doubt the credibility of the witnesses. An abbreviated version of their declarations follows:

1995—May 4, 1 sighting, 2 persons. Greg Ducan, publisher of the Stanstead Journal, *with Peter Ellis. . . . The sighting lasted 45 seconds to 1 minute. They were at the pier situated at Harvey Bay. This sighting was recorded on May 23, 1995 on a radio-cassette . . . Greg related his experience in his newspaper: "I saw Memphré, I am not kidding."*

1995—May 21, 1 sighting, 2 persons. Alain Marillac and Jocelyne Beaulé from Montreal saw a bizarre creature at Magog Public Beach measuring from 20 to 30 feet in length.

We have their declaration on a radio-cassette plus drawings. The description is different since they were not at the same place when it appeared.

1995—July 19, 1 sighting, 2 persons. Melissa Hathaway and her stepmother Mona Hathaway saw at Prouty beach, Newport, in a few feet of water a snake-like creature. They saw the eyes. The sighting lasted five minutes.

1995—July 25, 1 sighting involving 5 persons. Jean-Noël Fortin with 4 other persons saw a three-humped object for a 2-minute period in Long Bay. They observed the creature for 2 minutes and were only at 150 feet. It left a pool of air bubbles after diving back into the lake.

1995—August 4, 1 sighting, 2 persons. Alain Marillac and Jocelyne Beaulé. . . . They saw a creature and recorded on a video at the same place as before.

We have a letter dated September 1st confirming it and the video was shown on the *Canal D (Mystères du Monde)* on October 27, 1995. The last sighting reported was on August 2, 2001, where two persons heard a big noise, looked in front of their boat to see something with humps coming towards their boat. It plunged into the lake 5 feet from their boat.

Our research concerns specially three types of creatures. First the sea serpent with humps, then the sea horse, last the alligator type. The sightings most often observed in the lake are definitely the sea serpent with humps.

Patterns of Cryptids Emerge

A study made by Bernard Heuvelmans (founder of cryptozoology), and part of which was published in *The World Atlas of Mysteries* in 1978 by Francis Hitchings, states that the major sightings in the world were made on the Eastern coast of the United States. . . . The largest number consists of sea serpent with humps in second place the sea horse. One must not forget that Lake Memphrémagog is indirectly connected to the Atlantic Ocean through the rivers Magog, St. Francis, and St. Lawrence.

Our society works equally for the protection of the environment and hopes that "Memphré" will become an important spokesperson on the subject. He could even be an informer if he had to. As Brian Britt of *CFCF-TV* was saying in a report on the 19th of June 1986, as he was scrutinizing the lake from the Promenade Memphrémagog: *"I am watching in case I would see my friend "Memphré"; even if I don't see him it's a lot more fun to talk about him than to see him."*

The late Doctor Bernard Heuvelmans was so kind as to give to me an inscribed copy of his book *Le grand serpent de mer.* The inscription reads, *"To my dear colleague dracontologist, Jacques Boisvert, this treaty on underwater Dracontology, with all my congratulations."* (signed) Dr Bernard Heuvelmans.

Dracontology is a branch of cryptozoology. I hope that "Memphré" will try to show himself for the 15th anniversary of the founding of "La société internationale de dracontologie du Lac Memphrémagog." (S.I.D.L.M.)

Ode to a Monster

You who read these lines do not hesitate to communicate with us if ever you were fortunate to see the gentle creature of Lake Memphrémagog. . . .

> *The Serpent ere now in the depths did roam*
> *Under Owl's Head to his cavernous home*
> *After digesting this horrible meal*
> *His snakeful majesty did out again reel,*
> *Next to appear to Uncle Ri Jewett*
> *In one of his visions that made him a poet.*

An extract from the poem *The Sea Serpent Legend* as written by Norman Bingham from the recited memory of Mrs. Mary Moore. Text appears as it did in William B. Bullock's *Beautiful Waters* (Bullock, Newport, 1926).

Sightings Provide Credible Evidence

Jan Sundberg

Jan Sundberg, a former journalist and current cryptozoologist, founded the Global Underwater Search Team (GUST) in 1997. Since then, GUST has been dedicated to hosting expeditions to seek out marine cryptids (undiscovered animals) and prove their existence. In this article, published on GUST's Web site, Sundberg focuses on the credibility of sightings. Many scientists argue that sightings are not concrete evidence that lake monsters exist. Sundberg counters that hearsay is a part of the human condition and that the thousands of eyewitness reports should be given more credence.

Testimony about "lake monsters" and "sea serpents" is considered as no evidence by science and is called anecdotal evidence. Despite this, people can either be sentenced to life imprisonment or execution on anecdotal evidence alone (principal witnesses). In the past five years people have asked me over and over again why cryptozoologists in general and GUST in particular have gotten so meager results? Well, one of the reasons is certainly the lack of scientific backing, and this is so only because we rely on anecdotal evidence.

By disregarding witnesses we are told that we will be more critical towards the subject and what follows on that is rejection, a conclusion there is nothing to search for and a wrap-up that led us nowhere.

Scientists Devalue Anecdotal Evidence

In the past thirty-some years scientists and their advocates constantly refer to first-person testimony dismayingly as anecdotal evidence. They tell us that these are just stories that are of little use in ascertaining the truth.

They want us to believe that a person's firsthand experiences and testimony about them are of no merit.

They want us to believe that a scientist's observations are of utmost importance but that the common man's testimony is of little or no value. . . .

What we need, the scientists tell us, are numerous double-blind studies, trials, reviews, charts, statistics and publication in scientific journals in order to establish the veracity of sea serpent sightings.

The scientist bases his argument on the fact that double-blind studies are more reliable than first-person testimony because his results are reproducible by other scientists at any laboratory throughout the world.

The theory holds that experiment "A" is performed in New York and produces "A+B=C" results. If experiment "A" is performed in Chicago, Miami, Los Angeles, Stockholm, Hong Kong etc. the scientists should produce the same results as the experiment performed in New York, as long as they strictly adhere to the protocols of the experiment.

High Priests of Truth and Wisdom

Scientists tell us a person's word is of little use but they want us to believe their word. They are the self-appointed high priests of truth and wisdom. We must look to them for all the "important" answers in life. They try to set themselves apart from the rest of us because they adhere to more exacting standards.

What I see is age-old human nature at play. Fallible men and women desperately trying to bolster their importance and egos by saying that only they have access to ultimate truth.

If anybody is under the illusion that science is a dispassionate, objective search for truth and new ideas, I have news for you.

The history of science is one of entrenched protectionism of the status quo. The leading scientists of every generation dogmatically reject any new innovators because it often contradicts what they have been saying for the last couple of decades.

Genius Has Always Been Persecuted

We don't have to go all the way back to Galileo's persecution to see it. In the mid 1800's physician Ignaz Semmelweis was vilified for advocating hand washing after surgery. In 1879 Thomas Edison and his Carbon Arc lights, 1903 the Wright brothers and powered flight, 1912 E.L. Mole and the tank, 1926 John Logie Baird and his crazy invention, the television set.

These men and dozens more over the last hundred years have been ridiculed and ostracized by mainstream science. They were branded charlatans and fools for advocating ideas that were considered impossible by the canons of science of the day.

The reason all great innovators and visionaries are publicly crucified by mainstream scientists is because their ideas often contradict the ideas held by establishment scientists who have much invested in the established order. It's a massive blow to the egos for them to have to admit that they have been wrong for 20 or more years.

Albert Einstein, who must have agreed with laymen and [scientists] alike, once said, "Great spirits have always found violent opposition from mediocrities".

The fact remains that human knowledge is built largely on the testimony of people from ages past. The bedrock of information is the exchange of ideas and experiences by people from many different cultures, from family, friends and teachers.

History, newspapers, our legal system are all heavily reliant on reliable first-person testimony. We do not need scientists with all their agendas, egos and double-blind studies to know when somebody is telling us the truth, especially about a life-threatening disease. If your relative, friend or acquaintance tells you they have been diagnosed with cancer, you know that they are telling the truth.

If they tell you that they are going to try an alternative treatment and six months later they are cancer free, you know that it is a very high probability that the alternative treatment had something to do with it. When thousands of other people swear by it, we know it works for some people.

Of course people lie and deceive for a variety of reasons. But when you have dozens of independent testimonies from people with no motive for lying saying the same thing, it demands, at the least, a more thorough documented investigation.

Thousands of people have stated that there are unknown animals in both freshwater lakes and the sea. But still mainstream scientists tell us it is worthless; just like the television set and the airplane, right?

Chapter 2

Fact or Fiction?

The Monsters
Are Illusions

Distortion of Light Explains Lake Monster Sightings

W.H. Lehn

Until monster hunters can produce concrete evidence in the form of an animal carcass or live specimen, they mainly have to rely on eyewitness sightings. In a report in *Science*, a scholarly journal, W.H. Lehn, an electrical engineer at Canada's University of Manitoba, argues that atmospheric light refraction may cause a common object, like a stick, to appear as a creature to the human eye. When the conditions are right, an object at the surface of a body of water can look distorted. Lehn believes that many sightings may be a result of this phenomenon. Lehn's article is considered a classic in the study of lake monsters because he is a reputable scientist writing on a topic some consider unscientific and his theory is sound and has yet to be disproved.

Lake monsters have been a part of legend among many peoples. Modern sightings, too frequent to be ignored, have intrigued many scientists, with the result that the subject of lake (and sea) monsters has become the focus of some serious research. [Nessie scholars Rupert] Gould, [Roy P.] Mackal, and others have collected enough careful reports from reputable eyewitnesses to dispel any doubt that the observers were indeed seeing unusual phenomena.

Lake Monster Sightings May Be Light Distortions

The one element missing from all of these reports (with the exception of Mackal's brief and somewhat incomplete appendix on mirages) is any consideration that the observed or photographed evidence might have been optically distorted by the atmosphere. It may well be that many sightings of monsters can be explained as the sighting of a distorted and hence unrecognized image of a familiar creature or phenomenon.

In the same way that Mackal carefully weeds out much "evidence" as representing standing waves, birds, otters, and so on, it may be possible to accomplish some further weeding-out on the basis of image distortion.

Conditions Necessary for Distortions

It is well known that approximately horizontal light rays are refracted slightly downward, toward the denser layers of the atmosphere. This refraction can become strong enough to cause visible distortions if a temperature inversion is present to steepen the density gradient near the earth's surface. Very interesting cases arise when the temperature gradient is nonuniform with elevation. A single point on the object can then be the source for several rays, all entering the observer's eye at different vertical angles. The eye assumes that the rays entering it are straight; hence the observer perceives such a point as several points at different elevations. When there is a continuum of many rays passing from the single object point to the eye, these image points appear to coalesce into a vertical line. The resulting vertical distension of features within this zone generally distorts them so much that they become unrecognizable.

Reports Reflect the Conditions

A great many of the reports of monster sightings describe atmospheric conditions that are ideal for generating distorted images. Several relevant points are discussed in the following paragraphs.

According to [Peter] Costello, monsters are frequently reported in Loch Ness, Scotland, as well as "in many other steep-shored lakes in the cold temperate regions of the Northern and Southern Hemispheres, roughly in a band on either side of the 10°C isotherms." The surface water temperature of such lakes is usually well below that of the air for the first half of the year, since the warming of the lake lags significantly behind the air temperature. Hence a temperature inversion near the water surface is virtually guaranteed for much of the time during the spring and summer months. Nighttime pooling of cold air draining down the slopes will further strengthen this inversion. The notion that surface temperature inversions are correlated with monster sightings is supported by Mackal's analysis of Loch Ness data: of 249 sightings, only 31 were made at air temperatures below 13°C. Also, of a similar number of sightings, 77 percent were made in May through August—the month when the lake temperature lags the air temperature. Mackal states that the surface water temperature rarely reaches 15°C at the height of the warming; during spring and early summer the surface water is much colder.

More Connections

The steep shores that Costello mentions are not strictly necessary. The spring and summer inversions over prairie lakes (Lakes Manitoba and Winnipeg, for example) serve admirably for the generation of distorted images. Lake Manitoba is even reputed to have its own monster, Manipogo.

Another interesting correlation arises from Mackal's summary of lake surface conditions: 84 percent of the Loch Ness observations describe the lake as being calm or having only small ripples. Mackal is quite correct in stating that "disturbances at the surface are much easier to detect when the surface is otherwise calm." However, such conditions are also best for developing the strong shallow conduction inversion necessary for transmitting stable but distorted images.

Many of the sightings involve observer elevations close to the level of the lake itself—with the observer near the shore or in a boat. The distances along the line of sight are often of the order of 1 km or more. Either or both of these conditions require low, nearly horizontal light rays to pass from object to observer. Exactly these rays are most easily (and noticeably) deflected by refractive anomalies in the air.

Many different shapes are reported for the monsters seen in any particular lake. This is not surprising if some of the sightings are indeed distorted and unrecognizable images of different though familiar objects. Conversely, similar objects distorted in different ways would also result in different descriptions.

Distortions Can Appear to Be Moving

The type of motion described in many of the sighting reports is consistent with observation of refractive effects. Within a stationary inversion layer, the nature of the transmitted image is quite sensitive to variations in the observer's elevation. The image can undergo a large vertical shift in response to small vertical movements of the observer. Further, under the right conditions, inanimate objects can appear mobile even if the observer himself is stationary. If the inversion layer is in slow motion, perhaps containing wavelike undulations, the image can grow, shrink, or move about. It can also appear and disappear without a sound or a ripple, as many of the observations describe. Such undulations can impart a sinuous appearance to an otherwise straight horizontal object. Possibly some of the reports of sinuous neck and body movements can be attributed to this effect.

Confronting a Sighting

Of the many hundreds of observations, only one will be summarized here. The observation was made by H.L. Cockrell in the fall of 1958. Cockrell had spent several nights on Loch Ness in a kayak, hoping to photograph the monster at night. At dawn, at the end of his third night on the lake, the breeze suddenly dropped and left the lake surface mirror-smooth. As [Nessie hunter Tim] Dinsdale quotes Cockrell,

> Something appeared—or I noticed it for the first time—about 50 yards away on my port bow. It seemed to be swimming very steadily and converging on me. It looked like a very large flat head four or five feet long, and wide. About three feet astern of this I noticed another thin line. All very low in the water; just awash. I was convinced it was the head and back of a very large creature. It looked slightly whiskery and misshapen.

Cockrell managed to take two photographs before a slight squall passed over the lake, and the object appeared to sink. After the squall had passed, he again saw something on the surface, but this time the object proved to be a floating stick, 4 feet long and 1 inch thick.

Mackal conjectures that the entire experience was the result of fatigue and "tremendous psychological bias," although this does not explain why the squall would inter-

forth between the ends of the lake to make a seiche. It can take 4 days for the wave to go the entire 60-mile length of the main part of Lake Champlain.

A Seiche's Turbulence and Debris Can Create an Illusion

What does this have to do with lake monsters? Skeptics of the Champlain and Loch Ness monsters argue that this powerful, but unseen wave throws stuff lying around on the bottom of the lake up to the surface. This might make an old log appear to jump out of the water or move across the surface. A moving log could resemble a living creature from a distance. Skeptics also point out that most sightings of the Lake Champlain monster occur during the summer. While some of that may be the result of more tourists at the lake which increases the chance of somebody observing the creature, it is also the time of year when the seiches are most likely to occur.

So far nobody has been able to prove that the water monsters in these lakes are giant waves. Either way it is safe to say that something big lies under the surface at both Loch Ness and Lake Champlain.

Otters Account for Silver Lake Sightings

Joe Nickell

In this article, Joe Nickell, author of sixteen investigative books in which he has explored mysteries such as that of the Shroud of Turin and UFO phenemona, has turned his eye to the Silver Lake monster of New York. In the 1800s, Silver Lake was host to a lake monster. Amidst the sensationalism that developed, it was claimed that the monster was a hoax. Citizens of Silver Lake had allegedly created an artificial lake monster in an attempt to draw tourists to their town. In a strange turn of events, Nickell attempts to debunk the claim that the Silver Lake monster was a hoax. Nickell argues that the mechanism that was supposedly constructed to pull off the hoax never would have worked. He details early sightings and explains that he believes people really saw something. He suggests that people may have just mistaken common otters for a lake monster.

O n the night of July 13, 1855, in Wyoming County, New York, two boys and five men were fishing from a boat on Silver Lake near the village of Perry. After several minutes of watching a floating log, one man exclaimed, "Boys, that thing is moving." Indeed, according to the *Wyoming Times*, after bobbing in and out of sight, suddenly, "the SERPENT, for now there was no mistaking its character, darted from the water about four feet from the stern of the boat, close by the rudder-paddle, the head and forward part of the monster rising above the surface of the water. . . . All in the boat had a fair view of the creature, and concur in representing it as a most horrid and repulsive looking monster."

Soon, others were reporting sightings, and excitement spread far and wide. As reported in an 1880 pamphlet, *The Silver Lake Serpent*, "People came on foot, by carriage, on horseback, and in fact, by any means of locomotion in their power, to see if even a glimpse of the monster could be obtained, and the hotels found they had 'struck a bonanza.'" Several expeditions were launched—ranging from a whaleman with a harpoon to a vigilance society of men armed with guns to a company having a capital stock of one thousand dollars and bent on capturing the creature.

This was all to no avail, and the excitement eventually died down. Then, reports a [1984 book, *The Legend of the Silver Lake Sea Serpent*]: "Several years later [1857] a fire broke out in the Walker Hotel. Firemen rushed to the scene to put out the blaze. When they worked their way into the attic they came upon a strange sight. In the midst of the flames they saw a great green serpent made of canvas and coiled wire." States another source: "The truth was then revealed by Mr. Walker himself" who "built that monster serpent with his friends to pick up the business at the Walker House Hotel."

Building a Lake Monster

Mr. Walker was Artemus B. Walker (1813–1889), and the scheme attributed to him and "a few of his intimate and trustworthy friends" is described in a local history by Frank D. Roberts in 1915:

> The serpent was to be constructed of a body about 60 feet long, covered with a waterproof canvas supported on the inside by coiled wire. A trench was to be dug and gas pipe laid from the basement of a shanty situated on the west side of the lake, to the lake shore. A large pair of bellows such as were used in a blacksmith shop, secreted in the basement of the shanty connected to that end of the pipe, and a small light rubber hose from the lake end to the serpent. The body was to be painted a deep green color, with bright yellow spots added to give it a more hideous appearance. Eyes and mouth were to be colored a bright red. The plan of manipulating the serpent was simple. It was to be taken out and sunk in the lake, and then when everything was ready, the bellows were to be operated and air forced into the serpent, which naturally would cause it to rise to the surface. Weights were to be attached to different portions of the body to insure its sinking as the air was allowed to escape. Three ropes were to be attached to the forward portion of the body, one extending to the shore where the ice house now stands; one across the lake, and the other to the marsh at the north end; the serpent to be propelled in any direction by the aid of these ropes.

Roberts adds that "Many nights were spent" in the construction of the creature, after which it was transported to the lake one night and sunk at a depth of some twenty feet. Then came Friday evening, July 13, 1855, and—you know the rest of the tale. Today, Perry's city limits signs sport a sea monster, and the town annually hosts a lighthearted Silver Lake Serpent festival—most recently featuring hot-air balloons. . . .

The Possibility of a Hoax

The hoax story is a colorful yarn, but is it true? It has certainly been reported as factual even by writers inclined to promote mysterious monsters—providing a touch of skepticism that seemed to enhance those writers' credibility. For example John Keel's *Strange Creatures from Time and Space* claims the case proves "that a sea serpent hoax is possible and was possible even in the year 1855." Keel also claims that "witnesses generally gave a very accurate description of what they had seen." He is echoed by Roy P. Mackal whose *Searching for Hidden Animals* specifically states that the Silver Lake creature was "described as . . . shiny, dark green with yellow spots, and having flaming red eyes and a mouth and huge fins." Other sources follow suit, including the *History of Northwestern New York*, which states that watchers "beheld a long green body, covered with yellow spots . . . and a large mouth, the interior of which was bright red." Alas, these writers are merely assuming people saw what Roberts's description of the fake serpent indicates they should have seen. In fact, not one of the original eyewitness reports mentions the yellow spots or the red mouth.

Contradictions in Details

Among the problems with the hoax story is that—although wonderfully skeptical—it exists in a suspicious number of often-contradictory variants. For example, whereas Roberts's previously cited account of the hoax's discovery refers to a wire-and-canvas monster being found by firemen in the hotel attic, other sources give a very different explanation, stating that "in the debris left by the fire were found the remains of the Silver Lake Monster" specifically "the frame of the serpent" or maybe just "remnants of wire and green canvas."

At least one source asserts that "The creators of this stupendous hoax soon afterward confessed," and monster hunter Mackal names the "confessed" perpetrators as Walker and *Wyoming Times* editor Truman S. Gillett. However, one writer attributes the newspaper's alleged involvement to "rumor," and a long-time local researcher, Clark Rice, insists that Walker was only suspected and that "No one ever admitted to helping him."

Due to the many variations, the story is appropriately described as a "legend," "tale," or even "the leading bit of folklore of Perry and Silver Lake." States Rice: "It was a subject that was bantered around when you were growing up, and everyone had a different version."

The Hoax Was a Hoax

Invariably the books and articles that give a source for the tale cite Frank D. Roberts's previously quoted account. Writing in 1915, sixty years after the alleged hoax, Roberts gives no specific source or documentation, instead relying on a fuzzy, passive-voice grammatical construction to say, ." . . to the late A. B. Walker is credited the plan of creating the Silver Lake sea serpent," having supposedly been assisted by "a few of his intimate and trustworthy friends"—who, alas, remain unnamed. He adds, "It is said that the serpent was made in the old Chapin tannery"; further indication that Roberts is reporting rumor.

Never mind the alleged laying of the "gas pipe," when gas lines did not come to Perry until 1909 nor piped water until 1896, raising questions about the availability of the pipe. And never mind the "small light rubber hose" that reportedly extended from shore to serpent, when the availability of that seems equally doubtful in a mid-nineteenth-century village. There is a large old bellows, attributed to the hoax, that is displayed in the Pioneer Museum at Perry, but its display card states only that it is "believed to have been used to inflate the Silver Lake sea serpent."

Materials aside, the complexity of the alleged contraption as described by Roberts provokes skepticism. Although such a monster would not seem to preclude the laws of physics the propulsion method Roberts describes raises serious questions. The three ropes that were reportedly attached to the serpent and extended to three lakeside sites would have greatly complicated the operation, not to mention multiplying the danger of detection.

Indeed, the Silver Lake contrivance would seem to have been a rather remarkable engineering feat—especially for a hotelier and some village friends. One suspects they would have sewed a lot of canvas and made many experiments before achieving a workable monster, yet Roberts claims theirs worked on the first attempt. In fact, over the years attempts to replicate the elaborate monster have failed.

It Could Not Have Worked

Despite the claim that Walker created the serpent, 1855 newspaper accounts make clear that there was an earlier Indian tradition about a Silver Lake serpent and that, furthermore, such a monster had been "repeatedly seen during the past thirty years." Certainly, not all of the 1855 sightings can be explained by the monster contraption Roberts described. According to his account it was installed near the northern end of the lake, where both the inlet and outlet are located. Yet on Thursday, August 16, farmer John Worden and others who were "on the west shore of the lake between two and three miles above the outlet" reportedly sighted "the monster" about a quarter mile distant. Surely no one imagines the fake monster being controlled from more than two miles away! Neither can the monster apparatus explain sightings of a distinct pair of creatures at the same time.

In fact, the earliest version of the hoax tale appeared in the December 12, 1860, *Wyoming County Mirror.* "Everyone remembers," stated the brief article, "that during the Silver Lake snake excitement, at Perry, the hotel there reaped a rich harvest of visitors. A correspondent of the *Buffalo Commer-*

cial says that when about two years and a half ago, the hotel was partially burned, a certain man discovered the serpent in the hotel." This "was made of India rubber," and supposedly "corresponded minutely" with a *Buffalo Republic* description of the serpent. The man who discovered the rubber fake "has just got mad at the landlord and divulged the secret." The newspaper story ended on a skeptical note: "We suppose this last game is just about as much of a 'sell' as the original snake."

In sum, the historical evidence diminishes as we work backward to the alleged hoax, whereas, conversely, details of the story increase the further they are from the supposed event. Therefore it appears it was the story—rather than the serpent—that became inflated. If Walker and/or others did perpetrate a hoax, it is unlikely to have involved an elaborate contraption such as Roberts described.

Newspapers Contribute to Hoaxes

There were hoaxes associated with the 1855 frenzy but they were largely played out in the newspapers of the day, which treated the whole affair as great sport. For example, in September the *Chicago Times* reported that two visitors had seen the monstrous serpent harpooned and towed to shore. The newspaper jocosely reported that at nightfall the creature uprooted the tree to which it was tethered and returned to the lake. It was recaptured the next day, said the *Times*, whereupon it "awoke, threw its head 60 feet into the air; lurid eyes glared like balls of flame and its tongue, like flashes of forked lightning, 10–12 feet long, vibrated between its open jaws."

Insinuations of hoaxing probably elicited an early statement by *Wyoming Times* editor Gillett. On August 8, 1855, he wrote: "We assert, without fear of contradiction, that there is not a log floating on the water of Silver Lake—that nothing has been placed there to create the serpent story . . ." and that the paper had published what was related by truthful people.

Explaining the Sightings

Even if there was a hoax (either a fake serpent or a journalistic scheme), that does nothing to explain the earlier sightings. At this late date [in 1955,] we can only round up the usual lake-monster suspects. As the perpetual saga at Scotland's Loch Ness demonstrates, "monsters" may be created by floating trees and driftwood, leaping fish, swimming otters and deer, windslicks, and many other culprits—often seen under such illusion-fostering conditions as mirage effects and diminished visibility. For example, some of the Silver Lake sightings, including the one that launched the 1855 frenzy, occurred at night when visibility would have been relatively poor and imaginations heightened.

The Monster Could Be Otters

Eyewitnesses typically insisted the object was a living creature, sometimes with its head above the water. A possible candidate is the otter, which "when swimming seems a very large creature." While treading water, an otter can raise its head and neck well above the surface and otherwise simulate a monstrous serpent, especially if swimming with one or two others in a line. The large North American otter (*Lutra canadensis*) inhabits "virtually the whole of the New World." On one of my visits to Silver Lake, I was startled while walking along a nature trail to glimpse a creature swimming in a nearby stream; it quickly vanished and I was puzzled as to its identity until I later learned that otters had recently been reintroduced there.

I subsequently talked with New York State wildlife experts about otters possibly being mistaken for mid-nineteenth-century "lake serpents." Bruce Penrod, Senior Wildlife Biologist with the Department of Environmental Conservation, stated it was "very probable" that otters were in the Silver Lake area in 1855. And if the sightings were not hoaxes, he said, he would clearly prefer otters—or even muskrats, beavers, or swimming deer—over sea monsters as plausible explanations for such sightings.

His view was echoed by Jon Kopp, Senior Wildlife Technician with the department. Kopp had an illuminating story to tell. In 1994 he was involved in banding ducks and was sequestered in a blind on Lake Alice in Clinton County. It was dark, when suddenly he saw a huge snakelike creature making a sinuous, undulating movement, heading in his direction! As it came quite close he saw that the "serpent" was actually a group of six or seven otters swimming in single file, diving and resurfacing to create the serpentine effect. "After seeing this," Kopp said, "I can understand how people can see a 'sea serpent.'"

I thought of otters especially when I studied two previously mentioned accounts of 1855 that described a pair of "serpents" estimated at twenty to forty feet in length. Possibly the witnesses in each case saw two or more otters, which, together with their wakes, gave the appearance of much longer creatures. All of the witnesses were observing from considerable distances—in one case through a spy glass—distances that could easily be overestimated, thus exaggerating the apparent size of the creature. Because otters are "great travelers," with nomadic tendencies, it is possible that a group of them came into Silver Lake in the summer of 1855 and later moved on, thus initiating and then ending that particular rash of sightings.

It Was Not a Real Lake Monster

The least likely explanation for the Silver Lake reports is that some exotic creature inhabited its waters. Whatever people did see, the situation was hyped in turn by the local newspaper and the antics of would-be monster hunters. People's expectations were thus heightened and that led in turn to misperceptions. Even the overly credulous paranormalist Rupert T. Gould admitted that people expecting to see something could be misled by anything having a slight resemblance to it. Gould called this tendency "expectant attention" and it is the basis of many paranormal claims—apparently including sightings of the Silver Lake Serpent, a case of the tale wagging the monster.

The Nessie and Other Lake Monsters Are the Products of Weak Minds

Ronald Binns

In his book *The Loch Ness Mystery Solved*, Ronald Binns offers his solution to the enduring mystery. Binns has visited the loch since the 1960s and studied the evidence that has emerged over the last fifty years. In short, the solution he offers is that the Loch Ness monster is imaginary. He argues that, in the midst of the modern world, human beings need an enigma like Nessie, just as humans in the past created myths to comfort their anxieties. In the following article, Binns focuses on how the sightings in the 1930s may have been influenced by popular culture of the time and why the time was ripe for a monster sighting to spur the sensationalism that resulted. He notes that no concrete evidence supports the hypothesis that a large animal lives in Loch Ness. More pointedly, he levels a personal attack on monster hunters. He says that they are unscientific and unaware of their overly productive imaginations. Finally, he predicts that sightings will continue to arise, because, in his opinion, they are the result of human imagination, something that will never disappear.

Mankind has been fascinated by water since the beginnings of time. In primitive societies water was associated with the world of spirits, and many rivers and lakes had their gods.

Water comprised another, separate world: its surface mirrored the known world of *terra firma*, but its depths were dark, impenetrable, mysterious. It is probably this pagan tradition which lies behind the old Highland belief in water-horses and water-bulls. . . .

Myth in the Modern Age

In the last half century [1934–1984] water has lost much of its traditional romance and mystery. In the age of skin-diving, submarines, sonar and underwater photography, the marvels of underwater life have become the common currency of television documentaries. Loch Ness, with its black peat-filled depths and inaccessible shores, provides a suitable terrain for the last, great modern myth. . . .

Victorian Sensationalism

Each year a handful of individuals visit Loch Ness and have the good fortune to see a 'monster', very often without even intentionally looking for one. They are probably unaware of

just how much their behaviour mirrors that of their Victorian ancestors. The Victorians were very much aware of sea-
serpent sightings, and discussions of this mysterious and
elusive creature were common in the English press between
the 1840s and 1880s. What was more, the Victorian middle-
classes enjoyed spotting 'sea-serpents' with great frequency
at coastal resorts all round Britain. (This is surely what the
mysterious Miss Woodruff was *really* doing on the end of
the Cobb at Lyme in John Fowles's *The French Lieutenant's
Woman:* she was watching for a sea-serpent, and only in-
vented her lieutenant so as not to appear foolish in the eyes
of her Darwinian admirer, the 'serious' Mr Smithson.) . . .

The public interest in sea-serpents waned considerably
towards the end of the [nineteenth] century. Nevertheless
the line of descent from the great sea-serpent enigma down
to the Loch Ness monster is not hard to trace, helped on its
way by such romantic real-life adventures as the Gobi
Desert expeditions of the 1920s, which brought back the
first dinosaur eggs. Tennyson's much-anthologised poem
'The Kraken' gives acute expression to that haunting sense of
the marvellous which mythical deep-water beasts can in-
spire, while the idea that prehistoric monsters might actually be alive and well and living in remote corners of the
world was given popular fictional expression in Arthur Co-
nan Doyle's *The Lost World.*

The Effect of Monster Movies on Collective Imagination

The birth of the movies soon saw films taking over the ter-
ritory of the fantastic and bizarre which had previously
been the province of science fiction. The 1924 version of
The Lost World set the fashion for trick-photography and in-
genious mechanical monsters. It is probably no coincidence
that the Loch Ness monster was discovered at the very mo-

ment that *King Kong*, the masterpiece of the genre, was released across Scotland in 1933. Indeed, when Rupert Gould came to interview that all-important star witness Mr Spicer [an early eyewitness of the Loch Ness monster], Gould casually referred to the diplodocus-like dinosaur in *King Kong*. Spicer breezily admitted that he, too, had seen the film, and that his monster had 'much resembled' the one Gould had mentioned. Significantly the rediscovery of the Loch Ness monster in the nineteen-fifties coincided with a flood of monster movies, including *The Creature from the Black Lagoon, The Phantom from 10,000 Leagues, Monster from the Ocean Floor,* and *The Beast from 20,000 Fathoms.*

A Unique Conjunction of Factors

This, then, is the real 'tradition' which lies behind the Loch Ness monster, as opposed to the bogus sightings tradition. . . . What is fascinating about the monster is how its initial credibility depended on a unique conjunction of factors. The announcement of a monster in 1930 flopped; the announcement of a monster in 1933 proved a dazzling success. It is relevant to ask why. The immediate answer seems to be that in 1930 the weather was poor and no-one who lived around Loch Ness seemed ever to have heard of, let alone seen the monster. But in 1933, just as the story was once again about to die, a London tourist who happened to be in the area at the time the subject was being first aired in the local press, had a frightening experience with an otter on a lonely road. This tourist, Mr Spicer, subsequently wrote a melodramatic letter to the *Courier*, which treated his 'sighting' as a major news item. This in turn inspired a tiny handful of other sightings by impressionable teenage girls, passing tourists, and local eccentrics like Commander Meiklem. Ironically some of the more recent studies of the monster have begun to express reservations about land sightings by witnesses like Spicer. What they appear not to realise is just how much the whole legend of a monster depended on the timely appearance of Spicer's letter in the local press.

James Froude, the Devon historian, remarked some years ago: 'Once possess people with a belief and never fear, they will find facts enough to confirm it.' In the summer of 1933 the Loch Ness environment was peculiarly favourable to monsters (something which is borne out by the sightings statistics over fifty years). It was, significantly, one of the hottest summers of [the twentieth] century. Conditions for mirages and distortions due to heat-haze at Loch Ness were perfect. Moreover its waters were actually full of bobbing black tar-barrels, thrown in by workmen doing road repairs along the entire north side of the loch. In these circumstances the growing 'reality' of the monster is not entirely surprising, egged on as it was by Alex Campbell's anonymous promotion in the local press and afterwards assisted by such partisans of the sea-serpent as Philip Stalker and Rupert Gould and leg-pullers like Hugh Gray and Dr Wilson. . . .

No Concrete Evidence Has Surfaced

And so the Loch Ness mystery was given a new lease of life, and the monster myth has survived to the present day. But the paradox remains. Still no-one has been able to produce a convincing piece of movie film of the creature which witnesses have claimed to see. [A.C.] Oudemans's massive volume on the sea-serpent opened with the stirring words:

> Voyagers and sportsmen conversant with photography are requested to take the instantaneous photograph of the animal: this alone will convince zoologists, while all other reports and pencil drawings will be received with a shrug of the shoulders.

That photograph was never taken. Likewise after fifty years of highly publicised effort the Loch Ness investigations have got nowhere, and conclusive proof of the beast's existence is as far off as ever.

In a sober assessment of the zoological difficulties which a 'monster' raises, Adrian Shine has commented:

> The presence of an adapted marine fish-predator within the loch is not, in itself, particularly remarkable. What is remarkable is that it seems to be an unknown animal. Furthermore, some of its 'characteristics' raise difficulties no matter what class of animal is considered. . . .

As Shine frankly admits there are sound reasons why the monster cannot be a plesiosaur, or an amphibian, or a reptile, or a mammal: 'The least unlikely solution would be a fish. . . . Unfortunately, most sighting reports do not seem to describe a fish.'

Perplexed by the scientific question marks which the monster mystery provokes, Shine finally concludes: 'If we have any faith in human nature, then the sheer volume of testimony from Loch Ness justifies the search.' It is at this point that Shine's argument breaks down, for as we have shown the monster myth had its origin in some very dubious 'testimony' indeed, and the volume of eye-witness sightings over half a century is considerably smaller than anyone has previously realised. Moreover, recent research into the psychology of perception has cast grave doubts on the reliability of individual eye-witness evidence.

The procedures adopted by most writers on the monster, carefully selecting the 'evidence' to fit a pet theory about the beast's true identity, are circular and self-verifying. The eye-witness evidence and the photographs are so varied that they could fit a dozen different types of 'monster'. In reality they fit none. In truth, no single imaginary 'monster' could possibly account for the muddled and contradictory 'evidence' which has piled up at Loch Ness.

To psychologists the human fascination with monsters is

not hard to explain. People *like* believing in monsters; they make the world a more colourful and exciting place. As children we all live in a fantasy world and invent all kinds of imaginary beings. . . .

Most of us are able to give up our imaginary creatures, but a few individuals cannot. In retrospect what is striking about the Lock Ness story is the extent to which it has depended on a tiny handful of enthusiasts and star witnesses. Figures like Mr Spicer, Greta Finlay and Torquil Macleod have achieved an importance in monster lore which seems out of all proportion to the merits of their 'evidence'.

Psychologists would argue that some people do indeed 'see' monsters, but that the monsters are not actually creatures of flesh and blood but a projection of internal anxieties. This is borne out by the accounts of those who have suffered from depressive illness. . . .

Such experiences are, thankfully, perhaps rare. It does nevertheless seem significant that there should be such a strong correlation between sightings and mirror-calm conditions at Loch Ness. When the loch is a *mirror* it reflects, perhaps, images from the unconscious. Certainly the Loch Ness myth fuses some very potent psychological motifs: a serpent-like monster or dragon from another age, which both repels and attracts; an abyss of unknown depth; and a magic lake of impenetrable darkness. As [Argentinian writer Jorge Luis] Borges remarked, 'There is something in the dragon's image that appeals to the human imagination. It is, so to speak, a necessary monster.'

Monster Hunters Are Unaware of Their Real Motives

Monster-hunters can never quite bring themselves to admit what their jumbled motives are in devoting their time to the pursuit of a mythical beast. When pressed on the subject they usually talk in highminded tones about the great need for 'conservation' of these wonderful and rare animals. Nicholas Witchell has solemnly urged that it is the 'vital responsibility' of Her Majesty's Government 'to warn that any interference with the animals will not be tolerated.' There is something slightly absurd and comical about such tender concern, in view of the monster's astonishingly elusive nature.

Psychology is not something the believers care to know much about. It is the great monster hunt that matters, the agonisingly suspenseful wait for the next dramatic sighting, the next blurred snapshot. Paradoxically, far from doing anything to conserve their 'monster' the believers have merely attracted worldwide attention to it, and encouraged a crass, vulgar commercialism to invade the loch's shores.

In their fascinating but little-known sociological study of the monster Roger Grimshaw and Paul Lester conclude that,

> The quest after the monster might appear to the militant sceptic a burlesque of previous culturally accredited monuments of human heroism, exploration and discovery. It, in fact, reflects to a degree at least the contraction of the frontier of earthly explorational mysteries. At the same time it goes some way towards satisfying an individualistic thirst for exploration, adventure and detection. It is worth noting also the obvious affinities which exist between our monster entrepreneurs and that other archetype of western individualism and investigative enterprise—the private detective.

The analogy is an apt one, since monster-hunters do tend to be solitary individuals, chasing after the solution to a mystery in the face of a hostile world. Often they have had no formal education, and they revel in their amateur status. One day they know that they, the outsiders, will be proved right. They look forward with anticipation to the great day when the professional zoologists will be humbled.

The force which drives the monster-hunters on seems to involve much more than the simple pleasures of amateur detection. The Loch Ness mystery has now taken on some of the overtones of a fringe religion, with witnesses and faithful believers. Tim Dinsdale has often talked of his 'crusade' against scepticism and 'battle' against indifference. The favourite metaphors employed by the monster fraternity are religious and military ones. The main 'enemy' is establishment science—the zoologists of the museums and universities and other government-funded institutions.

In reality this conspiratorial scientific establishment is largely a fiction of the monster-hunters' own devising. Since believers themselves cannot agree about whether their monster is reptile, mammal, vertebrate or invertebrate, and without any hard data to go on, it is difficult to know what scientists are expected to *do*. John Napier, M.R.C.S., I.R.C.P., D.Sc., Visiting Professor of Primate Biology at Birkbeck College, London, has tartly observed:

> It has become a boring cliché of the monster establishment that scientists are afraid that the frailties of their own doctrines would be exposed should they so much as admit the existence of unknown animals or unknown forces.

> On the contrary, I have found that nothing intrigues a scientist more than monster tales. Most of my colleagues in Britain and the United States delight in speculating on possible theories, and often come up with ingenious solutions that seem to owe more to science-fiction than to the principles and methodology of science. This is the stuff of which coffee-breaks are made, and I can assure the monster establishment that their suspicions are quite without foundation. If there is a conspiracy of silence it derives at best from scientific caution, and at worst from sheer ignorance of the issues, but certainly not from a desire to hush up the truth.

Scientists can scarcely be accused of ignorance of the issues at Loch Ness. Many of them seem in fact to have had a good idea of what was going on, right from the beginning.

Believers never tire of quoting the case of the coelacanth, an archaic fish discovered to be still alive off the coast of

South Africa. The implication of its discovery, they hint, is that scientists can be wrong and that creatures supposedly extinct for 70 million years can still survive. But the case against living plesiosaurs rests on the fossil record. Scientists are unlikely to deny the survival of a species out of mere prejudice, not least because many species still extant such as crocodiles and turtles are known to have been contemporary with the dinosaurs. Monster-hunters also shut their eyes to one rather obvious fact about the discovery of the coelacanth. The first coelacanth was caught in 1938 and, although decomposed, was instantly recognized as such. A second specimen was captured in 1952 and a short-lived mystery was over. The relatively short period of time which elapsed between a coelacanth being first observed in the ocean, and a number of others being trapped and identified (seventy, at the latest count [in 1983]) is in marked contrast to the long-drawn-out Loch Ness saga, in which a hypothetical species of giant-sized animal has eluded even credible photographic 'capture' in a relatively tiny area of water. . . .

Search for Loch Ness Monster Is Unscientific

Throughout its fifty-year existence the Loch Ness saga has been a matter for enthusiastic amateurs, cheerfully ignorant of zoology, natural history, human psychology or even the history and ecology of Loch Ness itself. The kind of rigour and questioning attitude which any academic discipline properly encourages is alien to the monster-hunters. They are people who *know*, and anything which contradicts their faith is to be brushed aside. So convinced of the monster's existence are they that the believers have never even bothered to scrutinise the dubious origins of the mystery, or the bogus sightings 'tradition' erected around it. Nor do they seem aware that an immense creature fifty or sixty feet long which swims at high speed in pursuit of fish would be remarkable in other ways than just its elusiveness or monstrous appearance. The bigger and more active that animals are the more energy they burn up and the more food they require. . . .

Loch Ness monster addicts are, apart from being incurable optimists, incurable romantics. A 'sighting' is to them something almost akin to a miracle, an occurrence so rare that it is like (to quote one witness) 'the time of revelation'—something which exerts an often benign, strangely spiritual influence upon the observer. The effect has also been noted on those who have seen flying-saucers. Not for nothing is Loch Ness a place of pilgrimage, and the monster a creature whose very existence depends upon the word of 'witnesses'.

Fear and Insecurity Explain Witnesses' Certainty

Many people cannot accept that seeing *isn't* always believing. To doubt your own cognitive faculties is to disturb your own sense of yourself. The individual's sense of personal security can be put at risk and shaken by this recognition. The urge to prove that all these people who have seen monsters were right stems, in part, from fear and insecurity. . . .

The great appeal of the Loch Ness mystery is perhaps the way in which it offers everyone the chance to become an amateur sleuth, pore over the evidence, visit the dark mysterious waters, and concoct a new theory about what it is which has baffled the world for so long. The Reverend [Donald] Omand may have exorcised Loch Ness, but the enigma is surely not yet over. There will be more dramatic snapshots, more amazing eye-witness testimony, maybe even a snatch of movie film of something dark and ambiguous, churning away into the far distance. After fifty years one conclusion about the mystery can reasonably be drawn. There is no scientific evidence whatsoever of monsters in Loch Ness, and a handful of individuals will go on seeing them there.

Poorly Planned Expeditions Lead to False Conclusions of Monster Activity

Kurt W. Burchfiel

People have been sighting a monster in Lake Seljordsvatnet in Norway for the past 250 years. Kurt W. Burchfiel, a cryptozoologist, joined an expedition to the lake with the Global Underwater Search Team (GUST). In an article in *Strange Magazine*, Burchfiel details the events of the hunt. No monster was ever sighted, though some spotty photographs were obtained. Burchfiel denounces his experiences with GUST. He claims that GUST members are really just opportunists, interested in making quick money, not in scientific exploration. Burchfiel complains that poor scientists, like those that led the GUST team, ruin the credibility of cryptozoology as a discipline.

Legend has it that for the past two hundred and fifty years people have observed a large unknown aquatic animal frolicking in Lake Seljordsvatnet, a mid-sized lake located in the Telemark Province of Norway. While descriptions of the creature vary, it is generally described as serpentine or eel-like, ten to fifteen meters long, dark-colored, with a horse-like head that it carries above the water while swimming on the surface. The scant photographic evidence available shows only indistinct surface disturbances, some of which could be interpreted as humps.

Joining the Expedition

In April [1995] I learned from John Kirk of the British Columbia Scientific Cryptozoology Club of an expedition being organized to search for this alleged animal, locally referred to as the "serpent." Keen to put my interest in cryptozoology to practice in the field, I contacted the expedition's organizer, Jan-Ove Sundberg. Sundberg maintained several lake monster related websites including one devoted exclusively to his organization, the Global Underwater Search Team or GUST, and its planned expedition to Norway.

Promises Are Made

While I detected more than a slight degree of eccentricity in Sundberg during the course of my e-mail communications with him, on the whole he didn't sound unreasonable. His website seemed to indicate that he was at least familiar with some possible non-cryptozoological explanations for lake monsters, like the misinterpretation of known phenomena or the misidentification of known animals. He had succeeded in convincing some Scandinavian companies to loan him a wealth of high-tech goodies; a side-scan sonar, both a towed and a fixed echo sounder, a remotely operated underwater vehicle (ROV), a KonMap computer-assisted navigation system, night vision gear, underwater scooters for the divers, and access to top-of-the-line photographic analysis equipment. He claimed to have procured both a sizable research boat and a Zodiac semi-rigid inflatable. He had obtained financial backing from the town council of Seljord, the only village on the lake, that among other things provided free room and board for all team members. Most impressively, he informed me that the Discovery Channel would be producing a one-hour documentary on the search and a film crew would accompany us for the duration. With some reservations, mostly concerning the near complete lack of concrete non-anecdotal evidence in support of the "serpent," I signed-on. While I recognized that a genuinely scientific search was probably too much to hope for, it appeared as though the effort would at least be conducted in an informed and educated manner. It was heartening to learn that a noted British marine biologist, Dr. Jason Gibb, would be joining the team as would recognized Irish fortean [paranormal or unexplained phenomena] researcher, Dave Walsh.

The Expedition Could Benefit Cryptozoology

I did not go to Norway with the expectation of finding a lake monster, although I do generally accept the possibility that such things might exist. To my mind the relative success of the search did not depend on a positive finding. A negative finding could be just as valuable. Seljordsvatnet is fairly representative of a good number of the some two hundred lakes world-wide that claim to host a resident beastie. I felt that knowledge gained there, especially regarding possible non-cryptozoological explanations for lake anomalies, could prove useful to lake monster research generally.

The events that transpired over the course of the first few days of the "expedition," and I shall use that term loosely from now on, led me to significantly alter my perhaps overly optimistic assessment of Jan Sundberg and his efforts. Before getting into the details of my misadventure, let me state without reservation that there was no evidence obtained during the search that could be construed by a reasonable person to be supportive of the existence of a large unknown animal or animals in Lake Seljordsvatnet. It was not, however, a complete waste of time. While the search may not have produced a monster, it did produce a valuable case study on how not to conduct a research expedition. It may also provide an allegory that speaks for some of the problems that plague cryptozoology generally.

Trouble from the Start

Almost immediately upon my arrival at the lake an obvious and pervasive lack of organization and planning set off alarm bells, particularly in regards to equipment. The much-lauded research catamaran turned out to be a scratch-built houseboat. . . . Even worse, it was festooned with cartoon-like computer generated pictures of the "serpent". Some of the promised technical gear was conspicuously absent, including the night vision equipment, the Zodiac semi-rigid inflatable, and the underwater scooters. What was on site, while impressive, was also obviously quite complicated and did not seem to lend itself particularly well to "monster" hunting. Company representatives were around for a day to assist in the set-up and to give cursory briefings on operation, but it was clear that analyzing any data that the instruments might collect would be extremely problematic for people lacking any prior experience.

During the first full day of searching with the gear my concerns were confirmed. . . .

The echo sounders were even more problematic. . . . While the manner in which these instruments displayed data was visually impressive, the images that they produced could be wildly misinterpreted if the operator didn't understand the basic science behind them. . . .

The difficulties with the equipment were compounded by the lack of any real search plan. While the lake was divided into five general search areas, there was no method to the way in which these areas were covered. The boat's driver more or less made things up as he went along. Hours spent searching haphazardly for a moving target with largely ineffective instruments quickly made the eight-hour shifts on the lake something to be dreaded. . . .

First Contact by Sonar

On the first watch of the search we did have a relatively strong contact that was picked up by both echo sounders. During daylight hours most of the fish seemed to congregate at around thirty meters depth. . . . The contact on the first day stood out because of its size relative to the other contacts (about 1.5 centimeters on the screen) and red color (red being relatively high on the density scale). To my mind it was probably a largish fish, but still worth sending-off to [marine electronics manufacturer] Simrad for a more detailed analysis.

Jan Sundberg unfortunately did not share this reserved attitude. On the right margin of both echo sounder displays is a depth scale broken down into ten-meter increments. Jan measured the 1.5-centimeter-long contact against this depth scale and saw that it corresponded to approximately fifteen meters. That evening members of the press were informed that we had made contact with a fifteen-meter object, a completely nonsensical interpretation of the data.

While the other members of the team learned not to become overly enthused about subsequent contacts made with the echo sounders (none of which were as impressive as the first one), Jan never really seemed to grasp the concept. In fact it is fair to say that his level of technical proficiency with the equipment was markedly below that of any other member of the team. I am not entirely sure whether this was the result of an actual lack of understanding, a proclivity towards mindless optimism, or something worse. I do recall one night when the film crew was on board trying to capture the essence of working out on the lake at night. Ordinarily, Jan neither drove the boat nor monitored the instruments. He preferred to remain forward with his camera. On this particular night, however, I recall him being filmed seated in the captain's chair, playing for the camera by simultaneously driving the boat while attempting to manipulate the echo sounder. He seemed hopelessly unaware that while he was steering the boat in circles because he had no understanding of the computer-assisted navigation system, he was trying desperately to rotate a joy stick control on the echo sounder console that could only be moved up and down or left and right. I never saw him attempt either task again.

Ulterior Motives

From the onset of the expedition my concerns about the lack of organization were compounded with my misgivings about Jan Sundberg himself. Perhaps predictably, Jan the person comes across very differently from Jan the e-mail message. It was difficult to define his motivations.

In one respect there was Jan the self-promoter and showman, paradoxically obsessed with providing the press with any evidence he could to buttress his image as a legitimate monster hunter while at the same time frightened by the thought of what they might find to say about him. This side of Jan came into focus on our first full day in Seljord during a press conference at the village's cultural center. As Jan came to the podium to deliver a prepared statement he was visibly shaken and frightened, much more so than I would have expected from someone who had already given numerous TV and radio interviews. The audience consisted of a reasonably-sized group of Scandinavian print media representatives as well as our film crew who were present to document the event. As he began to speak Jan stammered and mumbled to the point of being nearly incomprehensible. Suddenly, the documentary's director interrupted and asked if he could begin again. Something was not correct with the shot. This generated several outbursts from the reporters who observed that they were there to cover a press conference and not a film shoot. Unceremoniously most of them got up and walked out. Despite this rather unpleasant turn of events Jan appeared visibly relieved. Rather than having to face a confrontation with what seemed to be a pretty cynical group of reporters, he was able to get away with meeting just a few of the more congenial ones later on down at the boat for a quick tour and photo opportunity.

Questions About Credibility

Rumors soon began to circulate within the group as to why Jan had seemed such a wreck face to face with the media. I do not mention them here to vilify Jan Sundberg and I offer no proof of their veracity. I relate them only to illustrate some of the tensions that were already building within the group by the end of the first day. One story held that Jan had a history of publicly championing some pretty far-out theories regarding UFOs and that some of the reporters were aware of this. Some newspaper articles on the search even referred to him as a "UFO expert." He had allegedly been involved in searching for crashed saucers, had claimed to have experienced some sort of UFO encounter on Loch Ness in the 1970s, had conducted UFO-related research in the Seljord area, and had suggested to someone that UFOs may have been responsible for depositing the serpent in Lake Seljordsvatnet. Another suggested that he had run afoul of the authorities back in Sweden and was the target of some sort of criminal investigation. One held that after having successfully evaded paying income taxes for some time the Swedish version of the IRS had finally caught up with him. Paying up the back taxes and the fines had left him completely broke. Still another offered that Jan was being paid $25,000 by the Discovery Channel to organize and lead the expedition. This one came from a particularly convincing source. Regardless of the accuracy of these stories, the group's general impression seemed to be that the prospect of having to field questions from the media about his past and present motivations made Jan extremely anxious. It also seemed to some as though Jan Sundberg had more of a stake in finding evidence of a "serpent" than he was letting on. . . .

Preexpedition Agreements

Most ominously, there seemed to be Jan the man with a hidden agenda who seemed to be more concerned with selling evidence than with collecting and analyzing it. Upon arrival in Norway every member of the group was made to sign a contract which stated, "All documentation without exception must be surrendered to GUST for analysis and sale." It further provided that, "All photographic evidence from the expedition; still photography, camcorder video, and underwater video will, in the case of a sale to media or others, be shared equally between the team of twelve." While provisions such as these would not sound unreasonable in terms of some sort of business enterprise, the heavy accent on selling evidence seemed out of place within the context of a legitimate research expedition. My concern was with getting any evidence analyzed by competent experts and making it available for scientific scrutiny, not with selling it to the highest bidder. Tellingly, in one of my first e-mail conversations with Jan I asked what his plan was for quickly conveying any compelling evidence we might collect to the scientific community for proper analysis. Beyond having made arrangements for getting photographic evidence enhanced, his response made it clear to me that he in fact had no plan for obtaining scientific interpretation. In hindsight it seems as though it was Jan's intention from the start that the only people who would be given genuine access to any evidence would be those who were willing to pay for it.

Questionable Photos

The matter of peddling evidence came to a head at the start of the second week when Jan took some photos of a wave. I was on the boat at the time so I am familiar with the details. For some time prior to taking the photos Jan had been sitting at the front of the boat talking to Jason Gibb. In discussing the incident with Jason later on I learned that at several points during their conversation Jan had excitedly pointed out several surface disturbances. Jason's assessment that they were just waves or boat wakes had met with no resistance. After several days on the lake it was clear to most that surface disturbances could be deceiving. Boat wakes can last a surprisingly long time. In a narrow lake they can actually bounce off the shoreline and eventually return to the middle. When the two halves of the wake intersect they can give the impression of a dark mass rolling just beneath the surface. This phenomenon caught my eye more than once. Even routine wave action can be deceiving. As the wind blows down on to the lake's surface from the surrounding hills it can create some long waves that at first seem to have no obvious cause. Strange waves, boat wakes, tricks of light, and the knowledge that you are on an alleged monster lake can all combine to momentarily fool even the skeptical observer. You could pretty much see whatever you wanted to see.

After talking with Jan, Jason came into the cabin to see how I was making out with the instruments. Within a minute Jan was pounding excitedly on the window. He insisted that he had just managed to snap nine or ten photos of a large object moving just beneath the surface and trailing a wake. Jason and I saw the "wake" in question. There was absolutely nothing unusual about it and nothing to suggest that it had been caused by something moving below the surface. It was just another wave in a lake full of waves. Arne Thomassen, the boat's owner, saw nothing unusual either. . . .

Capitalizing on Pictures of a Wave

Later that day Jan formally suggested to the group that we should consider selling the photos. He had already been in contact with the *Daily Express* in England and a sixty-thousand Kroner deal was suggested. Response from even the more reserved members of the group was swift and severe. How could we consider selling something that we hadn't seen yet? How could we get the photos analyzed and interpreted properly if we rushed off to sell them? Why should we even be talking about selling evidence, if in fact the photos really constituted evidence? What paper would possibly agree to buy photos sight unseen? Why had Jan gone ahead and approached the media without first speaking with the rest of the team? All of this seemed to catch Jan off guard. His goals were clearly not shared by the rest of the group. He resolved that he would deliver the film to Kodak in Oslo personally and that we could discuss the matter again after seeing the developed pictures. Before leaving, Jan unsuccessfully tried to hit up the film producer and several team members for money to cover the expenses of going to Oslo.

Upon returning from Oslo Jan presented his pictures to

the group. As predicted, they showed nothing more than an unimpressive wave. He insisted that Kodak's "experts" had determined that the wave might have been caused by an object moving just beneath the surface, although no such object was discernible and there was no way to be certain. When Jason Gibb questioned just how expert the Kodak people were in analyzing and interpreting photos of water-related phenomena Jan responded that they had analyzed "thousands of photos just like this". When Jason suggested that there was a difference between developing photos and interpreting them, Jan reiterated that Kodak were the experts when it came to photos and that they knew what they were talking about.

Selling a Video

But there was more to discuss. During Jan's absence another team member had taken twenty minutes of video at long range of what appeared to be three v-shaped wakes moving around the lake. Although the cameraman himself (my roommate Ulf Burman) suggested that the wakes were produced by ducks, Jan launched into a push to sell both his photos and the video. This time he took a slightly different approach. The group was informed that money for gasoline had run out and that Arne Thomassen had been paying for it out of his own pocket for several days. The town council had already paid out more than twice the amount of money that they had initially agreed to and were unwilling to help. Arne had to be compensated. We could either each contribute or we could sell the photos and the video to raise the necessary cash. According to Jan it didn't matter if the pictures showed nothing but a wave. We would make no firm commitment as to their authenticity. The paper that bought them could make whatever claims it wanted to. We would simply remain non-committal. The collective horror of the group was obvious.

This was tantamount to blackmail. Either sell the ridiculous photos or fork over the money yourselves. Jan called for an immediate vote. Only one other member of the team agreed to try and sell the photos and the video. In the face of this rebuke Jan informed the group that he would copyright the photos, sell them himself, and pocket the money. I reminded him that the contract we had all signed made any evidence collected the property of the team and that the group's decision not to sell the photos did not mean that ownership of them simply defaulted to Jan Sundberg. His response to me was, "Well, then I guess we'll have to change the contract."

The Beginning of the End

This was the beginning of the end for me. While it had been clear for some time that Jan's interest in the expedition went well beyond the purely academic, I could not allow myself to be associated with a charlatan and a profiteer. It was time to bow out. The next day I announced to the group that to my mind the search had devolved into some sort of convoluted money-making scheme. Perhaps this is precisely what Jan Sundberg had in mind all along. Even though I doubted that the photos could be sold, Jan's decision to defy the group and attempt to sell them against our wishes placed everyone's reputation in jeopardy. I was simply not willing to sacrifice my integrity in order to raise money to pay for gasoline that Jan, as the team leader, should have adequately budgeted for in the first place. To claim to the world that this was a legitimate well-organized search was a lie. As to legitimacy, legitimate researchers don't sell their findings to tabloids. As to the level of organization, I had been to better organized pillow fights. It was clear that Jan had assembled a group of sincere, intelligent, and genuinely interested people for use as props in a drama staged to make himself a quick buck in the guise of a "monster hunter." I announced my resignation effective immediately and left. My friend Dave Walsh followed suit. (Dave Walsh's account of the expedition can be found at: http://www.nua.ie/blather/archives2/issue2no16.html.)

Sadly, my experiences with Jan Sundberg and GUST98 seem to provide an encapsulated view of the problems that confront cryptozoology generally. Like the search at Lake Seljordsvatnet, the cryptozoological world seems to be divided into three camps. First, there are the legitimate and well-intentioned researchers. While some may be quicker to believe in extraordinary claims than others, their overly enthusiastic approach rarely results in intentional deceit or falsification. Then there are the charlatans, pseudo experts, crackpots, and profiteers for whom concepts like the scientific method are utterly meaningless. For these wretched few, the notion that extraordinary claims require extraordinary proof can be replaced with the belief that extraordinary claims require extraordinary lying and the intentional misrepresentation of data to obfuscate their inherent lack of [credibility] and substance. Unfortunately these people are responsible for a good portion of the inaccurate information that is readily available to the general public. Finally there are the professional scientists, the zoologists, marine biologists, and anthropologists. While some of these people bravely risk ridicule from their colleagues to publicly comment on cryptozoological phenomena, most steer clear to avoid association with the aforementioned unscrupulous types. This is unfortunate because many of these people are probably intrigued by cryptozoology and they alone possess the technical expertise and grounding in hard science that the discipline oftentimes lacks.

No Evidence Found

Again, while I do accept the possibility of lake monsters generally I saw nothing at Lake Seljordsvatnet that even remotely suggested the presence of an unknown animal. While there is some anecdotal evidence of interest, it is heavily intertwined with local myth and folklore. Some of the local claims are echoed at reputed monster lakes worldwide: the lake has some subterranean link to the sea (there is no proof of this); the monster lives in underwater caves (we dove to investigate several of these reported caves but the only two found were hopelessly small, closet-sized affairs); the fish in the lake are abnormally large (again, there is no proof of this); the lake never gives up its dead (it does); scuba divers are afraid to dive the lake (I wasn't). The perpetuation and acceptance of these myths is not deterred by the lack of any proof in support of them. This certainly doesn't make the existence of lake monsters seem like more of a possibility.

If lake monsters do exist in some tangible form then they have apparently developed a highly effective means of avoiding human detection. Maybe they are nocturnal. If air breathers, they might have the ability to take in air at the surface through snorkel-like appendages. Perhaps they are highly sensitive to the presence of humans and time their surfacing to avoid contact. Their best defense against discovery, however, may be that it is people like Jan Sundberg who tend to go looking for them. If this state of affairs continues then concrete proof of their existence is sure to remain elusive.

Epilogue: Analyzing the Evidence

Some people are surprised that in this modern world quite a few people are still engaged in monster hunting. Cryptozoologists, those who study unknown or hidden animals, point out that many animals thought to be extinct, fictional, or completely unknown were discovered in the nineteenth and early twentieth centuries. Coelacanths, mountain gorillas, Komodo dragons, and giant pandas are all examples of animals thought to be imagined or extinct but were later discovered to be real. The world is still a large place, with many more species yet to be discovered, believers argue. Some of these species, including lake monsters, might yet prove to be in existence.

Critics respond that no surprising new species has been discovered since the first half of the twentieth century. Therefore, it is highly unlikely that undiscovered large animals, particularly those living in large lakes, would remain unknown. Surely, sooner or later a specimen, alive or dead, would have surfaced. To this date, no such specimen has been produced. This simple fact is enough for many scientists to dismiss the idea that lake monsters are alive and well.

One does not have to be a lake monster hunter or a scientist to develop an informed opinion on the matter. This book explores many perspectives related to the issue. A thoughtful reader can come to some conclusions through critical analysis of the arguments presented in this book. This epilogue will help you develop a strategy for critically analyzing arguments. In addition, more sources of information on lake monsters are available in the bibliography.

The Author

A good starting point is to gauge the credibility of the author of the article. Read the introduction and biographical information at the beginning of the article. What does this information tell you? Do the author's credentials seem credible? To be credible is to be worthy of belief. In the modern age of the Internet, where Web sites are available to anyone with the means to set one up, questions of credibility are important in your research. Was the article written by an expert in cryptozoology who has written many books on the subject? Or was it written by an amateur? Is the author a scientist with advanced degrees? Questions such as these can help you determine the credibility of the author. It is not difficult to establish the credibility of the author if you study his or her background. You may have to do a little research on your own. An Internet search may be a good place to start, but do not take the credibility of Web sources, or any sources, for granted. Scrutinize the author.

The Argument

After you have found out a little about the author and examined his or her credibility, it is time to turn to the text or article that you wish to evaluate. You can use a series of steps in your approach to critical analysis:

1. *Determine the main claim of the argument.* The main claim is the hypothesis or thesis of the article. If the entire article was summarized in one sentence, what would that sentence be? Sometimes it is easy to figure out the main claim of an argument. Often, writers include their main claims toward the beginning of an article, in the introduction, or shortly following the in-

troduction. Occasionally, a writer may save his or her main claim for the article's conclusion. Sometimes, you have to figure out the main claim on your own. For example, you may find yourself asking your parents for twenty dollars some day to buy a CD. In that case, your main claim is, "You should give me twenty dollars."

2. *Identify the supporting evidence for the main claim.* Supporting evidence consists of the evidence or reasoning that an author gives to back up his or her main claim. After determining the main claim for an argument, be sure that you list all the supporting evidence. In what ways does the author attempt to prove her/his main claim? For the example listed above, you might support your main claim (that your parents should give or lend you twenty dollars) with evidence. You might mention that you have gotten good grades recently, that you have done a lot of work around the house, and that it is important that you get this CD because all your friends have it.

3. *Evaluate the supporting evidence.* Some kinds of evidence may be more convincing than others. Take a look at the evidence the author has given to support the main claim and evaluate it. Does the author provide compelling evidence? What is the form of the evidence? Photographs? Did the author see a lake monster, or is he or she just citing someone else? Is the author's theory based on the scientific method? In your argument for a CD, your parents would probably think about your supporting evidence. They might be more impressed by your good grades and the work you do at your house than whether you need the CD because your friends have it. Obviously, certain kinds of evidence are more compelling than other kinds.

4. *After evaluating the supporting evidence, think about other explanations.* How else could the phenomena be explained? What other possibilities exist in relation to the question that the article's argument seeks to answer? In your quest for the CD, your parents might consider the fact that you are given ten dollars (even though you may feel that you deserve more) a week for an allowance. They may wonder what you have done with this money, if you want the CD so badly.

5. *Synthesize (put together) your results from steps 1 through 4.* After your thoughtful analysis of the article, what do you think? What is your conclusion? Your parents might think about your argument and come up with an alternate solution. They might decide that instead of giving you the money, they will lend the money to you and that you could pay it back over the course of the next month out of your allowance.

Now, let us use these steps to analyze Peter Costello's article on the Loch Ness monster from this book.

1. Determine the Main Claim of the Article

The main claim of Costello's argument becomes evident a few pages into it: He posits the explanation that the Loch Ness monster could be a long-necked seal and then goes on to support that argument. The opening of the article leads up to this point, and the conclusion sums up the main point, once again, that the "monster" is really a group of long-necked seals.

2. Identify the Supporting Evidence for the Main Claim

Costello's support for his argument begins before he even gets to his main claim:

1. He gives a list of explanations of the Loch Ness mon-

ster and then goes on to refute them. He does this in support of his main claim so that other people analyzing his argument will have a difficult time coming up with other explanations for the Loch Ness phenomenon.

2. Costello argues that the environment, a cold, deep, freshwater lake, suggests that the large, unknown animal is a mammal, specifically a seal.

3. He argues that the "monster" must be an unknown form of seal since no known seal has such a long neck.

4. He turns to photographic evidence to back up this theory, specifically in terms of the creature's head and neck.

5. He draws on eyewitness reports to draw comparisons between the characteristics of the seal and stories of humps on the monster's back.

6. He once again uses eyewitness reports to explain conflicting descriptions of the monster's feet and hide.

After laying the groundwork for his argument, and under the assumption that the main claim is true, he theorizes on aspects of the monster. He argues that seals grow to be around twenty feet long, that there are fifteen to twenty living in the lake, and that these creatures avoid contact with humans.

3. Evaluate the Supporting Evidence

Costello begins by eliminating other theories regarding the identification of the Loch Ness monster. The assumption that underlies the whole argument is that there is definitely some sort of unknown animal at the heart of the Loch Ness phenomenon. With this assumption in mind, he hypothesizes some general characteristics of the animal in terms of its habitat, the Loch Ness. Afterward, he incorporates both photographs and eyewitness reports into his argument. He assumes that in both cases the evidence is genuine, then explains how it fits the long-necked seal hypothesis.

4. After Evaluating the Supporting Evidence, Think About Other Explanations

The assumptions that underlie the argument that Costello makes leave big gaps in terms of his supporting evidence. While he anticipates some other explanations for the Loch Ness phenomenon, he always assumes that it is some sort of undiscovered animal. He does not make allowances that the phenomenon at Loch Ness could simply be floating logs or common animals such as otters or waterfowl mistaken in photographs or by eyewitnesses as a monster. In addition, while he discounts the plesiosaur theory because a reptile could not live in the cold environment of the lake, he jumps straight to the seal suggestion and ignores other explanations, including that the unknown animal, if one exists, could be a fish. While he does look at photographic and eyewitness evidence, he does not do so with a skeptical eye. His assumptions are that the reports he focuses on are believable. Out of the thousands of reports of eyewitness sightings and the many photographs that have emerged at the Loch Ness, Costello has quite an enormous pool of evidence from which to draw support for his argument. He could just be picking a few reports that fit easily into his argument and ignoring others that might conflict with it.

5. Synthesize the Results from Steps 1 Through 4

Costello's argument is not very convincing. It feels like he may be writing to someone who is predisposed to believe that some sort of strange animal exists in the Loch Ness. Ultimately, with no concrete evidence, Costello must assume and hypothesize. Yet he does not state his claim in the form of a hypothesis; he states it as a fact. The bottom line is that the underlying assumptions of this argument are too unstable.

Let us look at Ronald C. Binns's article on the Loch Ness monster.

1. Determine the Main Claim of the Article

The main claim for this article may not be as easy to identify as that of Peter Costello's. For one thing, Binns's article is lengthier. You might begin by stating what he is not arguing. Unlike Costello, he is not arguing that some strange monster exists in the Loch Ness. At the beginning he seems to take a different route than Costello. You might initially state the main claim for this article in this way: Lake monsters are the results of people's imaginations. Still, this may be confusing to some people. They may ask what you mean by people's imaginations. Binns focuses on three products or character-istics of the human mind: imagination, culture, and psychology. You might revise the initial statement of the main claim like this: Lake monsters are the result of our need for mythology, our popular culture, and our psychology. You may also include Binns's claim that investigations are not based on the scientific method. A final main claim for this article may look something like this: Lake monsters are the result of our need for mythology, our popular culture, and our psychology; there is no scientific proof of their existence.

2. Identify the Supporting Evidence for the Main Claim

1. Myth is important to human beings. The often cited example of Saint Columba is an example of this sup-porting evidence, in terms of the Loch Ness monster. You might think of how this relates to other examples in North America in which legends of Native Ameri-cans are cited.

2. Popular culture sensationalized sea monsters before and during the sudden interest in the Loch Ness monster.
3. A letter to a newspaper regarding a mistaken sighting spurred an interest in the Loch Ness monster.
4. No concrete evidence has been produced in the form of a photograph or a film.
5. Monster hunters choose to focus only on the evidence that supports their specific argument. They ignore all other evidence.
6. Psychologists argue that delusional people (for example, depressive people) think that they see monsters.

3. Evaluate the Supporting Evidence

What kind of evidence is Binns relying on? Most of it seems related to culture. The assumption underlying Binns's article is that no scientific basis exists that proves that the Loch Ness monster is real. With that claim in mind, he then explains how or why people might "see" the monster. In fact, he seems guilty of the claim he makes regarding monster hunters—namely, that they start with a theory and then pick only evidence that fits that theory. In particular, he focuses on culture (the world we create and are a part of) and psychology (the world inside us). At the same time that he refutes the existence of a Loch Ness monster, he also attacks the credibility of monster hunters, suggesting that they are delusional people whom psychologists see as abnormal.

4. After Evaluating the Supporting Evidence, Think About Other Explanations

One problem with Binns is his unfair attack on monster hunters. He makes broad generalizations and lumps all monster hunters into one category: amateur, delusional, daydreamers. A reader is left with the opinion that many monster hunters probably do not fit this description. It also leads one to believe that Binns, then, may be disregarding their side of the story from the beginning. Binns also disregards the entire body of photos, films, and eyewitness reports as mistaken or false evidence. A reasonable person might consider that the sheer amount of such evidence requires an explanation that makes more sense than suggesting that people are imagining, mistaking things, or hallucinating.

5. Synthesize the Results from Steps 1 Through 4

Binns has some good arguments in terms of the roles that culture and psychology play regarding lake monsters. In particular, his arguments concerning the role of myth, popular culture, and the media make a lot of sense in explaining the sensationalism that arrived along with the burgeoning interest in the Loch Ness monster in the 1930s. However, his arguments concerning monster hunters seem cruel spirited and biased. Also, Binns goes a little too far with his last line: "There is no scientific evidence whatsoever of monsters in Loch Ness, and a handful of individuals will go on seeing them there." There are hundreds, if not thousands, of sightings of the Loch Ness monster. While it may be convenient to Binns's argument to make it sound like sightings occur only among a fringe group of lunatics, it seems counterintuitive to his opening evidence that myth is an important component of human existence. Some parts of Binns's arguments are acceptable, but others are not.

You Try It!

Pick an article from the book and go through the steps. Use the following format:

1. State the main claim. (Summarize the article in one sentence.)

2. Identify the supporting evidence for the main claim. (Try and stick to the evidence that refers back to the main claim. Occasionally, an author may include some extra material.)
3. Evaluate the supporting evidence. (Is it credibile? Why or why not?)
4. After evaluating the supporting evidence, think about other explanations. (What did the author leave out?)
5. Synthesize the results from steps 1 through 4. (Come up with a conclusion.)

Organizations to Contact

The editors have compiled the following list of organizations concerned with the issues debated in this book. The descriptions are derived from materials provided by the organizations. All have publications or information available for interested readers. The list was compiled on the date of publication of the present volume; names, addresses, phone and fax numbers, and e-mail and Internet addresses may change. Be aware that many organizations take several weeks or longer to respond to inquiries, so allow as much time as possible.

British Columbia Scientific Cryptozoology Club (BCSCC)
e-mail: cryptozoologybc@yahoo.ca
Web site: www.cryptosafari.com/bcscc

The BCSCC is a North American organization dedicated to scientific exploration, research, and investigation of cryptids. The group encourages its members to participate in cryptozoological research in their locales. The BCSCC meets in various cities in British Columbia for formal and informal functions.

Centre for Fortean Zoology (CFZ)
15 Holne Court, Exwick, United Kingdom EX4 2NA
(44) 1392 424811
e-mail: info@cfz.org.uk • Web site: www.cfz.org.uk

Since 1992 the CFZ has served as an international clearinghouse for cryptozoological information, research, and investigation. The organization publishes a cryptozoological magazine, books, and articles. In addition, the CFZ funds cryptozoological expeditions.

Committee for the Scientific Investigation of Claims of the Paranormal (CSICOP)
Box 703, Amherst, NY 14226
(716) 636-1425
Web site: www.csicop.org

Since 1976 CSICOP has looked at claims of paranormal phenomena with a critical eye. The organization is involved in critically investigating all such phenomena (including claims of cryptids such as lake monsters) through its conferences, publications, and research. CSICOP wishes to bring an objective and scientific lens to bear in its investigations and analyses. Its list of skeptic organizations will be of interest to those looking to balance the views of pro–lake monster organizations.

Global Underwater Search Team (GUST)
e-mail: jan.sundberg@bahnhof.net
Web site: www.bahnhof.se/~wizard/GUSTeng03/
gust_omgust.html

GUST was founded by Jan Sundberg in 1997. The organization leads expeditions in different parts of the world searching for marine cryptids. In particular, it has concentrated on searching for lake monsters in Scandinavia. GUST is actively recruiting members on its Web site. In the future, GUST plans on offering lectures, courses, and seminars regarding marine cryptozoology.

International Dracontology Society of Lake Mempremagog
525 Verchères, Magog, Canada J1X 3K8
(819) 843-9936
Web site: www.memphre.com

Founded in 1986, the society is specifically centered around research and investigation of Lake Memphremagog's lake monster, Memphre. In particular, the society collects reports of Memphre.

International Society of Cryptozoology (ISC)
PO Box 43070, Tucson, AZ 85733
(520) 884-8369
e-mail: isc-rg@cox.net
Web site: www.internationalsocietyofcryptozoology.org

The ISC is an interdisciplinary community devoted to the scholarly study of cryptids. The organization publishes a newsletter and a journal, *Cryptozoology*, which are available for purchase through the Web site. The organization has been in operation since 1982.

For Further Research

Books

William Akins, *The Loch Ness Monster*. New York: Signet, 1977.

Chad Arment, *Cryptozoology: Science and Speculation*. Landisville, PA: Coachwhip, 2004.

Henry H. Bauer, *The Enigma of Loch Ness: Making Sense of a Mystery*. Chicago: University of Illinois Press, 1986.

Ronald Binns, *The Loch Ness Mystery Solved*. Buffalo, NY: Prometheus, 1984.

Elizabeth Montgomery Campbell and David Solomon, *The Search for Morag*. London: Tom Stacey, 1972.

Steuart Campbell, *The Loch Ness Monster: The Evidence*. New York: Prometheus, 1997.

Loren Coleman and Jerome Clark, *Cryptozoology A to Z: The Encyclopedia of Loch Monsters, Sasquatch, Chupacabras, and Other Authentic Mysteries of Nature*. New York: Simon and Schuster, 1999.

Loren Coleman and Patrick Huyghe, *The Field Guide to Lake Monsters, Sea Serpents, and Other Mystery Denizens of the Deep*. New York: Putnam, 2003.

Peter Costello, *In Search of Lake Monsters*. London: Garnerstone, 1974.

Tim Dinsdale, *The Leviathans*. London: Routledge, 1966.

———, *Loch Ness Monster*. London: Routledge, 1972.

———, *Monster Hunt*. Washington, DC: Acropolis, 1972.

Arlene Gaal, *In Search of Ogopogo: Sacred Creature of the Okanagan*. Blaine, WA: Hancock House, 2001.

Rupert Gould, *The Loch Ness Monster and Others*. New York: University, 1969.

Dennis Jay Hall, *Champ Quest 2000: The Ultimate Search Field Guide & Almanac for Lake Champlain*. Jericho and Underhill, VT: Essence of Vermont, 2000.

Paul Harrison, *Sea Serpents and Lake Monsters of the British Isles*. London: Robert Hale, 2001.

Bernard Héuvelmans, *In the Wake of Sea-Serpents*. New York: Hill, 1968.

F.W. Holiday, *The Great Orm of Loch Ness*. New York: Norton, 1969.

John Kirk III, *In the Domain of the Lake Monsters*. Toronto: Key Porter, 1998.

Joel Levy, *A Natural History of the Unnatural World*. New York: St. Martin's, 1999.

Roy P. Mackal, *The Monsters of Loch Ness*. London: McDonald and Jane's, 1976.

Nick Redferd, *Three Men Seeking Monsters: Six Weeks in Pursuit of Werewolves, Lake Monsters, Giant Cats, Ghostly Devil Dogs, and Ape-Men*. New York: Pocket, 2004.

Philip L. Rife, *America's Loch Ness Monsters*. Lincoln, NE: Writer's Club, 2000.

Karl P.N. Shuker, *The Beasts That Hide from Man: Seeking the World's Last Undiscovered Animals*. New York: Paraview, 2003.

James B. Sweeney, *A Pictorial History of Sea Monsters and Other Dangerous Marine Life*. New York: Crown, 1972.

Nicholas Witchell, *The Loch Ness Story*. Clinton, MA: Penguin, 1975.

Periodicals
W.H. Lehn, "Atmospheric Refraction and Lake Monsters," *Science*, July 13, 1979.

Web Sites
American Monsters, www.americanmonsters.com. This beautifully designed Web site specializes in cryptids of the United States, but has branched out to include monsters from all over the globe.

Committee for the Scientific Investigation of Claims of the Paranormal, www.csicop.org. CSICOP is a scholarly organization with a focus on careful scientific evaluations of mysterious phenomena.

CryptoZoo, http://cryptozoo.monstrous.com. This Web site hosts a wealth of basic information about cryptozoology and scientists involved in the discipline.

Global Underwater Search Team, www.bahnhof.se/~wizard/GUSTeng03/index.html. GUST is composed of a team of cryptozoologists led by Jan Sundberg. The organization's Web site offers details about GUST's monster hunting expeditions.

Lake Monster Culture, www.lakemonsterculture.com. This Web site chronicles a college graduate's year-long study of the culture of various locations connected to lake monster phenomena.

Monster Tracker, www.monstertracker.com. Home of the "Bessiecam," this simple site is dedicated to South Bay Bessie, Lake Erie's monster.

Museum of Unnatural History, www.unmuseum.org. This online museum chronicles the fringes of known science, including the subject of lake monsters.

Skeptic's Dictionary, http://skepdic.com. The dictionary offers skeptical sources to counter claims of paranormal activity. While it is not always scientific in nature, it offers a counterpoint to the many amateur cryptozoologist organizations.

Strange Ark, www.strangeark.com. Hosted by Chad Arment, an author of lake monster books, Strange Ark offers many important resources, including the BioFortean files, links to online cryptozoological print resources.

Strange Magazine, www.strangemag.com. This Web-based magazine publishes articles on many different kinds of strange phenomena.

True Authority.com, www.trueauthority.com. True Authority's mission is to provide balanced and logical explanations for cryptozoological mysteries.

Index

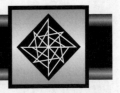